KARL RAHNER

MARY
MOTHER OF THE LORD

THEOLOGICAL MEDITATIONS

HERDER AND HERDER

HERDER AND HERDER NEW YORK

232 Madison Avenue, New York 16, N.Y.

Original edition "Maria, Mutter des Herrn",
Herder, Freiburg. Translated by W.J. O'Hara.

First edition: 1963

Second impression: 1963

Third impression: 1964

Nihil obstat: Carolus Davis, S. T. L.
Censor deputatus
Imprimatur: E. Morrogh Bernard, Vic. Gen.
Westmonasterii, die 30. Novembris, 1962

The Nihil obstat and Imprimatur are a declaration
that a book or pamphlet is considered to be free from doctrinal or moral error.
It is not implied that those who have granted the Nihil obstat
and Imprimatur agree with the contents, opinions or statements expressed.

Library of Congress Catalog Card Number: 63-8329
First published in West Germany © 1963 Herder KG
Printed in West Germany by Herder

CONTENTS

The eight chapters of this short work are the text of eight conferences given in the University Church of the Holy Trinity in Innsbruck during May devotions. They were preceded by ten others (given by another speaker), on the teaching of Scripture concerning Mary. That explains why in the present work, references to Holy Scripture are less to the fore, and why the mode of expression is more that of doctrinal instruction. Apart from polishing the style here and there, and making a few slight additions, I have left these discourses as they were delivered. That will be to their disadvantage. Perhaps, however, there are to be found in them some thoughts that have not yet occurred, at least explicitly, to this or that reader. The theme itself is, of course, inexhaustible, like all the realities that God's grace has effected for our salvation. The preliminary section (the Short Outline), was an addition, intended to furnish the reader with some relevant indications, that the talks themselves necessarily presuppose.

Karl Rahner

A SHORT OUTLINE OF THE TEACHING OF FAITH ABOUT MARY

I

MARY is the virgin Mother of Jesus Christ. The meaning of this statement, and the fact that it says everything about her, become clear, if one considers whose mother she is, and in what way she is his mother.

The Christian faith professes that Jesus Christ is the Son of God, equal and identical in nature with the Father, the Son of God who has become man. This requires brief elucidation. Christian belief has its own doctrine of the relation between God and the world. Both are genuine realities, quite distinct from one another. God's reality exists absolutely independently in itself, infinite, necessary, eternal, spiritual and personal. The world is a genuine reality, but dependent on God, because it arose through him by creation. It is now still running its course through time, and this temporal succession of its history has a definite direction, for it is orientated towards a final condition that will be its true fulfilment. The relation between these two very different realities is, however, in the specifically Christian view, not merely that of creation. Ultimately and decisively, the relation is determined by the fact that God not only creates the world to be distinct from himself – creation in the natural order – but creates it in order to communicate himself to it, with his own intrinsic reality, freely, – supernatural grace – and does actually communicate himself to it, – the world with the strictly supernatural mode of existence that "nature" has received. Consequently God himself comes forth from himself, and the world is drawn up into God's own life, in a process that will only be concluded when the world reaches its fulfilment. In the actual order of things, in which nature has been raised to the supernatural, God's primary intention, therefore, is really this communication of his very self, this will to give himself, and the "nature" of the world is the condition that grace prepares for itself even though it remains true, – grace remains grace, – that God could have created this natural world (of matter and mind), without communicating his own self to it. This communicating of himself, this drawing up of the world to himself by his loving self-giving, always takes place in the world in accord with the capacities of the individual beings that make up this world. It attains its true end, in accordance with its true intent, in the spiritual and personal creatures. Thanks to the unlimited scope of their receptivity in knowledge and love, which characterizes their very nature, they are capable of receiving directly God's communication of himself, in the proper sense of the term. if God gives himself freely and gratuitously.

In this history of God's gift of himself, it is mankind as a whole, and as a unity, that stands before God and is spoken to. This history is enacted everywhere and at all times, by the offer of grace to the free human being of every age, in every situation. But as well as the general, universal working of God's grace, it has a definite, historical identity – sacred history or history of salvation in the narrower sense – when God bears witness to his salvific will, by the revelation of his word, and by miracles, at certain points in space and time, and in their interconnections. Acceptance of this self-communication, addressed by God to the community of human persons, is an act freely elicited by a human being, and this act itself is produced by the efficacious grace of God who is giving himself. Consequently the history of the human being who receives God is, once again, one that praises the glory of his grace. Here too God creates for himself the condition for his self-communication, by grace, yet of course in such a way that this condition of God's intervention in the world really becomes the human being's own reality.

This self-communication of God is addressed to every spiritual creature; by sanctifying grace here in this world, and by the direct sight and love of God and the perfect possession of him in the next. Its real foundation, its ultimate peak, the seal set on it, its tangible manifestation in the history of our salvation, its irrevocable final phase, consists in God's becoming personally present in the world, by the Incarnation of the Word of God. Once this occurred, it was manifestly the intended apex of the whole saving work of God, in relation to which everything else in fact from the first was designed, as condition or consequence. Seen from God's side, the Incarnation is the means for the whole self-communication of God to the realm of created spiritual persons, while in the perspective of created realities, the Incarnation is the goal and summit of creation. The mystery of Jesus Christ consists in his really standing on both sides of the line that divides God from his creature in the purely natural order of creation. He is truly man, he has his own human reality, a human life and history, a human nature, in which the Word of God truly expresses himself to us. Consequently one has in very truth comprehended and apprehended something of God himself, when one apprehends something of this humanity. He is truly God, that is, the Word of God, in whom God as principle (the Father), in the communication of his own divine nature, – in the full self-expression which constitutes a divine person, and is not addressed to a creature, – expresses himself (the Son). Consequently the same person (the Second person of the blessed Trinity), exists as God, in the divine nature communicated to him by the Father, and in the human nature which he received, in time, from the virgin Mary.

Mary is the virgin mother of Jesus Christ. This relationship must not be understood narrowly, in a way that would limit it to a merely physical one. In faith and consent freely given – it too a gift to her from God's grace – she conceived for us the Son of God and in her womb gave him that earthly existence through which he could be a member of the new human race and consequently its redeemer. By reason of the hypostatic union of the Son of God with the human nature received from Mary, Mary is truly the "mother of the Lord" (Luke 1:43), mother of God (Council of Ephesus A.D. 431). Her divine motherhood is effected by her faith (Luke 1:43; 2:27 ff.), and so it is not a merely biological occurrence. Nor is this consequence of her faith an event that belongs only to her private life-history. It is the accomplishment of her divine motherhood, in other words the central event of the whole public history of redemption itself. For this divine motherhood occurs, by God's grace, as a freely-willed conception, receiving for the world the grace that the Incarnation brings; it is a true partnership with God's action for mankind. When Scripture (John 19:25–27) shows us Mary by the cross, under the tree of redemption, as simply the "woman" (the second Eve and the mother of the redeemed), we can see that the function of conceiving redemptive grace, which belongs to her as Christ's mother, was carried further by her, throughout her whole life, until the "hour" of the redemption (John 2:4). It is for this reason that she is also called "co-redemptrix", though this is a notion the full implications of which are still a matter of discussion in Catholic theology. Her rôle in the history of redemption (divine motherhood), and personal holiness (the blessedness that was hers because she believed),

13

coincide in her, one determines the other and they mutually correspond. On account of this central position of hers in the divine economy of redemption, whereby she conceived salvation for all, and for her own sanctification, she is, and the Church is ever more clearly and explicitly conscious of this belief, the absolute and radical case of the redemption of humanity. She is the person who was redeemed in the most perfect way, and so she is the prototype of the redeemed, and of the Church in general, comprised in the will of God decreeing the redemptive and therefore triumphant Incarnation of the Word of God.

By reason of this perfect redemption, Mary is preserved from the inherited guilt of original sin. (Immaculate Conception, defined by Pius IX, 1854.) For although she is a member of Adam's race and its community of guilt, she possessed sanctifying grace from the beginning of her existence, through the foreseen merits of Christ, because she was implied in God's decree to send the redeemer. For the same reason, being preserved by God's grace from every personal sin, she is without sin, as the Council of Trent teaches, and from concupiscence, that is to say, from limitation of moral freedom of control over the psychosomatic powers. That she conceived the Son of God without the operation of man is explicitly affirmed in Holy Scripture (virginity before the birth, Matt. 1:18 ff.; Luke 1:34–35). It is patent and manifest through this origin of her son from a mother but not a human father,

14

that with him a radically new beginning of salvation is made, not a continuation of the guilt-ridden history of mankind, though the latter is itself brought into the new by redemption. In the sense and to the extent that the element of hurt and pain in childbirth is, according to Genesis 3:17, a manifestation of the dominion of sin, Mary's childbearing was exempt from it. (Virginity in childbirth: common doctrine of the Church since the fourth century.) Because of the total dedication of her whole being and life to the exclusive service of God and Christ (see 1 Cor. 7:25 ff.), and this too in relation to the public history of the divine plan of redemption and the Church, of which Mary is the type, the Church professes that Mary was ever a virgin after the birth of Christ. (Tradition of the Church since the third century, fifth General Council, A.D. 553. The brethren of Jesus mentioned in Scripture were not Mary's children, but distant relations.) And since the history of salvation is already so far advanced in its final phase of transfiguration even of the material world (through the resurrection of Jesus; see also Matt. 27:52 ff.), the Church proclaims that Mary, perfectly redeemed, has already attained her complete perfection in body and soul. (Assumption of Mary into heaven; solemn definition by Pius XII, first of November, 1950.) Moreover, insofar as the heavenly intercession with God, on behalf of the communion of saints on earth, by those who have attained salvation, derives its foundation and significance from the function they performed, while on earth, in the divine economy of salvation, and which has now achieved eternal recognition and validity, Mary by her unique position in the history of redemption is truly the "mediatrix of all graces", not of course in the same way as Christ, who effects them, but ministering, interceding, and receiving.

II

LITTLE is known of Mary's life otherwise. The references in Holy Scripture are meagre: Luke 1–2; Matt. 1–2; John 2:1–2; Mark 3:31–35; John 19:25–27; Acts 1:14. What is related in apocrypha and legends of the second century has no historical value; at best it can only be considered as evidence of theological speculation about Mary, which has been given the form of an ostensibly historical account. That is how we must regard the reports about Mary's Assumption, dating from the fourth century. Otherwise there is nothing of any historical value in such apocryphal works. So, for example, we do not know the names of Mary's father and mother, and the story that Mary was a temple virgin is quite fictitious.

Scripture tells us she was a descendant of David, related to the priestly line of Zachary and Elizabeth, betrothed and married to Joseph of Nazareth. The angel Gabriel appeared to her in Nazareth for the annunciation, and there she conceived her child. (These events of the narrative of Jesus' infancy happened about the year 6 B. C. of our calendar. The return to Nazareth took place after the death of Herod I, who died in B. C. 4.) Mary shared the religious practices of pious people among her fellow-countrymen (presentation in the temple, circumcision of the child, pilgrimages to the temple), led a life of labour, poverty, and willing acceptance of the impenetrable decrees of God. During Christ's public life (starting about A.D. 27), she maintained, as Jesus wished, an attitude that shows that what is most important, even in her motherhood, is not the merely physical motherhood as such, but the fulfilment in faith of God's will. She recedes into the background, only to stand under the cross in the decisive hour of our Lord. After Christ's ascension, we find her praying in the community of the disciples. Nothing is historically known about the further duration of her life, or the circumstances of her death. But it cannot be doubted (though a few Catholic theologians have in recent times disputed it), that she did die, as the true completion of her earthly existence, sharing the common lot of mankind, and imitating the example given by the death of her Son. For, although sinless, she was to represent, not the glory of the earthly paradise, but the perfect victory of the grace of Christ in the weakness of the flesh, her sinlessness being, not an inheritance from the earthly paradise, but the fruit of Christ's redemptive death on the cross. She lived in the body, which is capable of suffering, and subject to suffering, and this is brought to its fulfilment by completing its suffering in death.

III

In accordance with the general possibility of Christian veneration of saints, and with Mary's unique position in the history of salvation, and in the community of the saints, who, sharing in God's blessedness, have perfectly attained the purpose of that history, Mary is to be called blessed by all generations (Luke 1:48). To honour God's work in her is in fact a unique way of praising and being grateful for the one great and comprehensive benefit that God has conferred on mankind. Besides, God's grace must be given recognition in what it has actually done, and in what the Scriptures reveal its work to have been. The special honour paid to Mary as the Mother of God, which of course has nothing to do with adoration, is called hyperdulia. This is simply the religious veneration due to those who are redeemed and sanctified in the complete sense, in heaven, – dulia –, but in the special case of the unique dignity of Mary as the Mother of God, and of her unique position and function in the divine plan of our redemption. Such religious honour, in other words, has its intrinsic basis and measure in the holiness and dignity of the person in question. The history of honour paid to Mary is that of the Church's growing awareness of her belief in the unique position of Mary in the history of salvation, in which everyone is dependent, not only on God, but also on the human beings, in whom and through whom as his "coadjutors" (1 Cor. 3:9), God effects our sanctification. Such growth in the explicit unfolding of what

Scripture itself already testifies concerning Mary is a phenomenon met with in regard to more or less all the truths of faith, and cannot be limited to the apostolic or sub-apostolic age, by anyone who believes in the vitality of the Church, governed in all ages by the Spirit of God. This honouring of Mary reflects, in the course of the centuries, continually new aspects of the blessed Virgin: her position in the scheme of redemption as the second Eve; her divine motherhood; her virginity as a model of virginal life in the Church, as type or figure of the "virgin Church"; the Mother of Sorrows at the foot of the cross; the Pietà; her motherhood; the type or figure of the Church itself; the mediatrix of grace; the mother of the spiritual life; the Immaculate Conception; she who is perfectly redeemed in body and soul. This veneration finds concrete expression in the Church through various feasts of the blessed Virgin, that celebrate individual events and mysteries of Mary's person and life, or relate to events in the history of the Church that have some reference to Mary; various prayers, the Hail Mary, the Memorare, the Rosary; pilgrimages to various shrines; consecration to Mary; the placing of individual religious orders and confraternities under her special protection, and so on.

Real and authentic honouring of Mary by confident prayer to her can be a measure of our success in moving beyond a general abstract belief in God and in actually achieving the concrete reality that Christian faith signifies. Such veneration of Mary fulfils the words of Scripture: "All generations shall call me blessed."★

★ The above outline of course could not consist entirely of propositions that embody defined truths of the faith, if it was to form a connected whole. Where it is a question of actual defined truths of Mariology in the strict sense, the relevant references are given to the pronouncements of the Church's magisterium.

MARY IN THEOLOGY

WHEN a Catholic wants to reflect more deeply on the mystery of the blessed Virgin, the first thing he does is to open Holy Scripture and see what it has to say about the blessed virgin mother of our Lord Jesus Christ. Not that this would be the first way he heard about her, for of course as a child on his own mother's lap he would have learnt the Hail Mary, and at catechism, that is, in the oral teaching of Holy Church, he would have been taught about Mary. When he opens the Scriptures, they are always for him the Church's book; he receives them from the Church, and reads them with her interpretation. This being understood, it is true to say that if he wishes to meditate more closely on the blessed Virgin, he first of all opens the Scriptures. For true though it may be that Holy Scripture can only be read correctly under the guidance of the teaching authority of the Church, yet conversely, Holy Scripture, by its inseparable connection with the Church and her teaching office, is a norm and standard for her faith and magisterium. The Church preaches what she reads in Scripture. And because she preaches precisely what she has read unceasingly throughout the centuries, we too can repeat what the faith of the Church keeps on affirming concerning Mary. That is why we can ask ourselves directly in these meditations what the Church herself in her preaching of the faith and her theology has to say about Mary. We know perfectly well that in so doing, we have, in effect, read the Scriptures with the Church, even when the Church's pronouncements, in their outward form of expression, seem to have a different ring about them from the words we can read directly in the New Testament.

Before we can ask in detail, however, what the Church tells us about Mary, in her preaching based on her own understanding of her belief, we can and must ask first, how it is that Mary figures at all in our faith, in the mind of the Church, and the preaching of the faith. Has faith anything at all to say about Mary? The question of course does not mean that we are calling in question the existence of the blessed Virgin, or casting doubt on what Holy Scripture relates about the mother of our Lord who is God and man in the unity of his person. That is not an answer to our question. Someone might say: Of course there is this virgin Mary, and this human life-story, narrated in the margin of Scripture. Of course there is this virgin, when it is the story of Jesus' private life more or less that is being told. Yet, they might continue, when faith is in question, when a man professes what he believes about God, on God's word, then it is the one God alone, and his grace alone, that is in question. For to do theology is simply to speak of God. A man then must only profess his faith concerning God, he cannot speak of every conceivable thing, however beautiful or fascinating, mysterious or exciting. It might be maintained that when faith is in question, nothing can be said except about God the most high, the thrice holy, the inexpressibly mysterious, God who alone constitutes our salvation and our eternity. It might be held that there is no room for anything else in preaching and theology. One might consider that everything else must recede into profound silence, however praiseworthy it might otherwise be, or deserving of reflection. One might think it only permissible to speak there of God, his grace and his redemption, and consequently of his Incarnate Word. It might be held that nothing more could be said about anything else in preaching and theology, than is said, for example, about Pilate, who also figures in the creed. Just as there are human beings who are named as it were in the margin of the creed, simply because in the history of the Word made flesh, they represent humanity's refusal of faith, so also, one might say, there may be persons mentioned in passing in marginal notes about the faith. They are named, to be sure, but are not an object of faith, of what it affirms, or of theology.

Consequently we must first answer the question: Is there any such thing as a theology of man? Only when we have answered this question can we boldly, confidently and joyfully enter the domain of faith and theology, in order – if it is possible to say anything at all about man – to say something about that human being who is the holiest, most authentic, and happiest human being, to say something of her who is blessed among women.

There is in fact a theology of man, a preaching of the faith and a theology that praises and glorifies God, by saying something about man. How is this? God is indeed really all in all. There is nothing beside him worthy of mention for its own sake, when faith is preached and theology pursued. In this holy house of God one cannot really speak of anything, praise anything, mention anything except the eternal God and him alone. Before him everything else sinks into the abyss of its absolute insignificance. There is not, in theology and in faith, God and then everything else imaginable as well, there is only the incomprehensible triune adorable God. When mind and heart are raised to him confessing their belief, all else must fall silent and be passed over in silence. Then there remains nothing for a man but to adore and praise that Godhead. For the life of faith and the endeavour of theology are of course one day to blossom into that one life whose entire content is the loving contemplation of God face to face, the eternal praise of his grace alone. And yet there is a theology of man himself, a confession of faith that says something about man himself, not in the margin of the profession of faith in the one eternal God, but comprised in it. How is this? Because God himself, in the life of the blessed Trinity, in his ineffable glory, in his eternal life, has taken us into this eternal life that is his. We do not need to be dead, as a poet of our day wrote, for God to live. He has not only given us something that he created out of nothing, something finite. Beyond all that, he has given us himself. He called us from nothingness, that we might truly be, he gave us freedom, that we might be able really and truly to be his partners, in his presence. He has made a covenant with us. He has not only willed to deal with us through the creation, where everything we meet with is always merely finite, a sign only, and a mere pointer to the God who ever remains beyond. He has willed to act directly with us himself, so that what happens, and what he does, what he shows and what he gives, is ultimately, in reality, himself, even if as yet only in the promise that he will one day reveal himself to us face to face, with nothing to stand between him and us any more. Further, – it is the most adorable mystery of faith – he has himself become man in the person of his Word.

Since that is so, and since it belongs to the mystery of our God that he is not only the God of the philosophers, but the God of Abraham, Isaac and Jacob, and what is more, the Father of our Lord Jesus Christ, who has become man, and our brother, it follows that for us Christians there is no acknowledgement in faith of the eternal God, unless we praise him for having given himself to us so totally, that we can proclaim with truth about one who is a man: he sitteth at the right hand of God the eternal.

25

Consequently no doctrine of God is possible any more without a doctrine of man, no theology without anthropology. It is no longer possible to say who God is in the full truth and reality of his actual life as he lives it, without saying that his eternal Word, in whom he utters and expresses himself, is man to all eternity. It is impossible now, here in Christendom, post Christum natum, now that Christ is born, to say anything true, genuine and concrete about God, unless one acknowledges him as Emmanuel, God with us, the God of our flesh, of our human nature, the God of our human sacramental signs, the God of our altars, the God who was born of the virgin Mary and consequently God and man in one person, a human being among us. Since this is the true, real living God, it is clear why the countenance of a man is seen within the sphere of divine faith and theology. For the same reason such a genuine theology necessarily, not merely accessorily, as part of its essential function, glorifies man, and can only praise God by so doing. That is ultimately why a mariology is possible, a teaching of the faith concerning the blessed virgin mother of our Lord. That is why mariology is not merely a piece of the private life-story of Jesus of Nazareth, of no real ultimate significance for our salvation, but an affirmation of faith itself concerning a reality of the faith, without which there is no salvation.

There is a further consideration. We human beings are important for one another. We mean something to one another, not only in the everyday things of life, not only because, (since we exist), we have parents, not only because, in the biological sphere, in the external life of the civil community, of art and learning, we are always dependent on a great human community. That is not the only reason for our importance for one another. Even in our salvation we are also similarly dependent on other human beings. That goes without saying, as a matter of course, yet it is difficult to grasp. One might think we were only important to one another for this life, for external things, or at most in the domain of the spirit here on earth. Or one might think that when it is a question of how God stands to me and I to God, of the ultimate decision about my eternity, of how I shall fare one day, when through the inexorable loneliness of my death, I stand utterly alone before the face of God, that then, in all that, I am absolutely alone and isolated. Then, surely, there is only the one God, and myself, his love and mercy, and my irreplaceable freedom in guilt and grace. Yet it is not so, for all that. All that has been said is true, but it is not the whole truth. For we still belong to one another, even then. Each has his own, inalienable, unique freedom, from which he cannot escape, which he cannot shuffle off on to someone else. But for all that, it is not a lonely isolated freedom, not even when it is deciding the eternal destiny of a human being, or making the fundamental choice of a human life. For the eternal Son, the eternal Word of the Father, was made flesh, born of the virgin Mary. In our family, out of our race that stretches from

27

the first human being, Adam, to the last, the Word of the Father was made flesh.

There is, therefore, a community in nature and in grace which takes effect in a community of sin and guilt, of the mercy of God and his grace, a community of origin and goal. But guilt and grace, origin and end, are God's concerns. Consequently the community of mankind extends into the domain of man's eternal salvation with God. It is a community in eternal welfare or loss, a vast community which acts out as a whole, and not only in individual human beings, the great drama of history before the eyes of God, and which brings to light what God's thought about mankind was. Only all these thousand and one varieties of men who, in co-operation or in conflict, form the one course of world history, together bring to realization what was really intended when God said in the beginning: "Let us make man to our image and likeness."

Since we belong to one another, not only in everyday life, in politics and secular history, but in the unfolding course of salvation, there is, then, a history of grace and salvation, in which we all belong to one another, and so none is without importance for the others, and all are important for each individual. Each must bear the load of guilt and grace, not only for himself, but also for all the rest. What one suffers, prays, weeps over, endures, and finds blessedness in, is of decisive importance for everyone, for the innumerable host of men and women who live that history. We belong together. But then, since it is God who is occupied with us in that history of grace, since our faith and theology must speak of him as the Lord of that one single history of humanity's eternal gain and loss, it again follows that man will have to be included in what faith has to preach and theology to state, for they are an account of God's saving work for us. And he has so disposed his dealings with mankind, that one human being is important for another there. He has simply willed that his redemptive work in us shall be effected by him through human beings. That is why the blessed virgin Mary must be included in what faith and theology have to say about those who are important in the divine plan of redemption. For she is the mother of him on whom salvation is entirely built, because he is God and man in one person. And Mary is also of decisive importance for our salvation's being found in Jesus Christ, inasmuch as this was given to her in God's unfathomable salvific will itself. She must have a place in theology. A doctrine of God involves a doctrine of man, and as part of it, a doctrine of Mary. In the midst of the praise faith gives to the one God of salvation, of the Incarnation, of grace, and of the one divine plan of redemption, what concerns Mary must be spoken.

What does all this signify for us? First and foremost, it means that Christian theology has something to say about man, that is, about ourselves. If we want to use for once the fashionable word, we can have an existential theology.

29

Nowadays there is a lot of talk about men. Even in philosophy, man is made the key to the interpretation of being and reality in general. Well, it is quite possible to say that when we are engaged in our May devotions, we are engaged in a Christian understanding of the human situation. It is God's word concerning us that we are there concerned with, a blessed and holy understanding of our own life. For there we are not seeing man merely as an ambiguous being, placed between two abysses of nothingness, nothing but anguish and distress. There we are speaking of Mary. We are praising her as blessed and holy, and by doing so, we are also, ultimately, saying something about ourselves. When we celebrate May devotions, we call nature to our aid to praise man as the image of God, to proclaim that he is redeemed, called by God into his own holy and blessed life. We are celebrating and proclaiming the Christian idea of man. In fact we are very up-to-date (if indeed we have any mind to be so), when we expound the old sacred truths we acknowledge every time we kneel and pray: And the Word was made flesh . . . born of the Virgin Mary.

Our reflections show us, furthermore, that we all belong together. We all share the burden and the blessedness, the danger and the salvation of all the rest. That of course is why we meet in this sacred congregation. A congregation praying, singing, and listening to the word of God, is not only an assembly of lonely, solitary people, not only a number of isolated individuals, who, impelled by concern for their eternal salvation, gather here for merely practical convenience, in order to try to work out their own private salvation for themselves alone. We are a holy community praising God by praising the glory of the blessed Virgin precisely because in our very salvation we are dependent on this virgin mother of God. We are a holy community, truly belonging together and therefore meeting together, truly experiencing in unity the grace of him whom God gave us by the obedience and the body of the blessed Virgin. We are those who have been called away from the loneliness and isolation of the individual into the unity of the love and grace of God.

So we must be in the everyday world too. We cannot pray here together if outside we cannot get on together in love and mutual trust, associate in mutual forbearance. Consequently, devotion to Mary is something that, by the very root from which it springs, has something to do with love of one's neighbour. For no doctrine concerning Mary could have importance and significance for us, if it were not true that each of us is responsible for the salvation of his brethren, and can and must intercede for them with prayer and sacrifice and aid. That is why Mary is not only the mother of our Lord, but our mother too. And so we have come here together to praise Mary once more at this time in the joy of our hearts. Such praise is ultimately praise of the eternal God himself, who in the person of the Incarnate Word has drawn near to us, when the Word was made flesh, born of the Virgin Mary.

THE FUNDAMENTAL IDEA OF MARIOLOGY

IN our first meditation we considered why faith and theology can have anything at all to say about a human being, seeing that their only subject is God and the work of his mercy to men. Now that we are going on to reflect on what faith affirms concerning Mary, we will not begin by thinking over separate truths about her one by one. We will try first to see the character and rôle of the blessed Virgin as a whole. By character here we don't mean anything psychological, a character sketch or anything of that kind. It is simply a matter of seeking a fundamental principle, from which the many truths of the Catholic faith concerning Mary, which we shall still have to meditate, follow self-evidently, – a basic statement to which one can return again and again when, exhausted almost by all the splendours of Marian doctrine, one wants to express quite simply and soberly, as it were for everyday use, the sum of what has been said about Mary, and is important for our own life.

Theologians, especially in recent times, have repeatedly

propounded this question to which we want an answer ourselves to-day. They seek a fundamental principle of systematic doctrine about Mary. We do not intend, in these brief meditations, to try to emulate this acute discernment of the theologians, if for no other reason than that they express their views in a great variety of ways; and we cannot make a choice out of this profusion. Some say that the decisive truth among Marian dogmas is that of her divine motherhood. Others reject this and maintain that it is not in itself sufficient, despite its undoubted historical priority as the first Marian dogma. For it could be misinterpreted to mean that Mary as mother stands in a purely private and personal relation to Christ as her physical son, whereas really this does not concern us, however great the dignity of such a divine motherhood may be. For that reason, attempts are made to elucidate and complete this oldest of Marian dogmas, so as to make it clear that Mary in a true sense is our mother too, because by her free consent (which the grace of God enabled her to give), she conceived her Son for the redemption of the world, and so played a decisive rôle in the history of salvation, and not just in the private life-story of Jesus. Or again they say that Mary is Jesus' mother and ours, mother of the whole Christ, head and members. Others prefer the formula, that to Mary belongs a universal motherhood. And yet again there are those who speak of a physical and a spiritual motherhood. Or they say that Mary is the second Eve, and, pursuing this parallel, with Christ as the second Adam, they follow the steps of the Fathers of the Church, as early as the second century, in trying to bring together all we know of Mary's function in the divine plan of redemption. Or they say that Mary is that person in the history of salvation who, in the name of mankind and as representing the Church, accepts and receives salvation for us all. Others again speak of a bridal motherhood of Mary in regard to Christ, so that she is not only his mother, but stands beside him as the bride of the divine Word, just as the first Eve stood beside the first founder of the human race.

In this and other ways theologians have tried time and time again to express the characteristic rôle of the blessed Virgin in a brief formula, so that the totality of what the faith declares concerning Mary may be to some degree present to the mind that ponders it devoutly. We will not try here to outdo all these efforts, nor undertake to select one of these suggestions as the best. We will take quite a straightforward, plain path, so as to answer the question of who exactly Mary is, from another angle. Of course, in order to do so, we must know a lot about her already. We don't need to act as if we didn't know it all, or had forgotten it. Of course we must know beforehand the goal that our reflection is to reach. But in order to attain it as a single and yet comprehensive goal, we will start with the widest general question of all, that will show us how Mariology fits into the structure of theology as a whole. Here is the question: What exactly is perfect Christianity?

What is Christianity? That is something quite straight-forward and comprehensive. Christianity is not something thought out or discovered by men. It is not man's approach to God by his own power. Nor is it primarily the fulfilling of commandments given us by God so that for our part we may observe them. Christianity is rather what the living God does in relation to us, what the living God of grace gives us, in forgiveness, redemption, justification, and the communication of his own glory. Since, however, what God gives is not, in the last resort, a created gift, but himself, Christianity is ultimately simply the eternal God himself, coming himself to a man, and himself by his grace influencing this man, so that he freely opens his heart for the whole glorious infinite life of the triune God to enter the poor heart of this tiny creature. This one total ultimate can be considered from God's side, and then it is God's love for man, by which he gives his own self to man. Or it can be viewed in human perspective, and it is man's love for God (given him by God), by which he accepts God's gift, which is God himself. Christ also said, of course, that such love for God in men includes love of the neighbour, so we must not forget our neighbour in this one ultimate. In the present connection, this chiefly means that the love of one's neighbour which is comprised in the love of God, also chiefly consists in our receiving the whole divine life by the power of God's grace, with faith and love, into the depths of our heart, in such a way that it extends and redounds to a blessing for others who by our side, like us, are to receive the one and only salvation from the eternal God.

What is perfect Christianity? What has been said makes it not difficult to give an answer. Perfect Christianity must consist in receiving this gift of the eternal God, God himself, in grace-given freedom, with body and soul and all the powers of the whole being, with all a man is and has, all he does and suffers, so that this receiving of God takes up his entire nature and his whole life-history into the eternal life of God. Perfect Christianity must mean that our public and our private acts, what appears publicly before the world in its history, and what takes place in the inner depths of conscience, perfectly coincide and correspond. What occurs there in the depths of Christian life becomes visible, and conversely, what is visible and manifest, truly mirrors what is taking place in the depths of the soul, in God's presence. Christianity in its perfection must also mean that this Christian's perfect Christianity unconditionally serves the salvation of others, and is only really perfect if it is actually devoted to all, from the beginning to the end of time.

If that is what perfect Christianity is, then we can and must say that Mary is the actual realization of it, the perfect Christian. If Christianity in its perfect form is the pure acceptance of the salvation of the eternal triune God that has appeared in Jesus Christ, Mary is the perfect Christian, the Christian human being exemplified as such, because in the faith of her spirit and in her blessed womb, with body

and soul, then, and all the powers of her being, she received
the eternal Word of the Father. If perfect Christianity is
the perfect correspondence between outward mission in the
history of salvation and personal life, it is perfectly realized
in Mary. She received visibly and tangibly the Incarnate
Word of the eternal Father, and so she is the most significant
and representative figure among the merely human beings
in the externally visible history of redemption. And at the
same time she accepted fully and realized in her personal
life her unique office in the economy of redemption, with
an absolutely unconditional total consent in faith. If
Christianity is the radiating influence of one's own grace
in unselfish service for the salvation of others, Mary is the
most perfect instance of what it means to be a Christian,
for it was the salvation of us all, Jesus Christ our Lord,
whom she conceived by the consent of her faith and in the
physical reality of her divine motherhood.

Viewed in this light, Mary is clearly the perfect Christian
and an actual typical expression of what redemption itself
in its most perfect form actually means. For that reason she
is the noblest of human beings in the community of the
redeemed, representative of all who are perfect, and the
type or figure that manifests completely the meaning of
the Church, and grace, and redemption, and God's salvation. She can rightly be called the second Eve. And if
Christianity means to receive God, not merely in some
abstract realm of thought, but in an actual historical context, in his Incarnate Word, in his world-transfiguring

grace, in short, in human flesh and blood, it is clear that the most perfect instance of such Christianity, of such a receiving of God in concrete human terms, is the divine motherhood, provided that this is not simply thought of inadequately, as a merely biological event, but is understood as something that involves the whole nature, body and soul, of the blessed Virgin.

A single yet comprehensive idea of the blessed Virgin therefore emerges from asking this question about the perfect Christian, who receives redemption in Jesus Christ. All that the faith says about the realization of redemption, about salvation and grace and the fullness of grace, is realized in Mary. This human person whom we call Mary is as it were the very point in the whole history of our redemption at which the saving grace of the living God descends from him into this history, and from which it is diffused over the whole of mankind. For her Son, whom she accepted in the strength of her heart, whom she conceived in faith and love, is the Redeemer of the world. And since, as Scripture testifies, the consent she gave in faith and obedience belongs not only to her private life-story, but to the public history of redemption, it must correspond, in harmony of person and function, to the purpose for which it was given; in short it must be perfect. In that case, however, the redemption of us all which comes to us in and through her, must be fulfilled and realized in her perfectly, at the absolutely decisive point in the history of salvation, for this latter always consists inseparably in a work that is both God's and man's through God's grace. Consequently Mary is redeemed in the most perfect manner, she is the finest result of the redemptive work of her divine son.

It follows too that Mary is one of us. We honour her, praise her, love and revere her unique dignity. We know that in a true sense (which we will consider later), she is a mediator on our behalf with Jesus Christ. But she is all that as one of us. Jesus Christ, the Son of the eternal Father, though a divine person, is also truly man, belongs to us as a human being. He is the second Adam, the spokesman of the whole human race, he is our brother and comes before his eternal Father for us and with us, in order to find there at the throne of grace, redemption and salvation for us. But because he is both God and man, and as such the mediator between God and man, he comes to us from God's side too. However truly he worships and pays homage to the Father with us, in virtue of his human nature, nevertheless he is also at the same time the God we worship as our eternal last end. His mystery consists precisely in being both. But if, in view of this mystery of her son, we ask, where does Mary stand? we must reply, she belongs entirely with us. She must receive God's mercy just as we must, for she lives and typifies to perfection what we ourselves are to be in Christ's sight. We shall never reach the incomparable holiness and dignity of this most blessed Virgin, for God distributes his gifts as he wills, and we cannot ask why he has given this to one and that to another. Yet, what Mary has, must in the ultimate resort be ours too. We too are to become what she is. She comes before God with us – like us and as one of our company – in the innumerable host of mankind. By doing this she is our mediatrix. In our midst, within the history of mankind as a whole, as a part of it, she accomplishes her own life-story, which takes on a unique importance for our salvation, and which, once lived through with this significance, endures eternally in God's sight. Only in this way is she our mediatrix, as we shall have to consider in more detail later. Precisely because Mary, in this position as intermediary, is entirely one of us, and only occupies that position because she belongs with us, as a mere creature, to the one human family, is she so near and dear to us. That is why we love her. And have an almost too merely human trust in her. And feel her intercession, protection and love to be so near and human, although, or rather because this dear and familiar humanity has been taken up, unimpaired and transfigured, into the eternal life of God himself.

So when we say without further ado that Mary has received God's saving grace (working through Jesus Christ and experienced in herself), in the most perfect way, for herself and for us all, we have expressed what the most holy Virgin is in herself and for us, in the most elementary concepts of theology, intelligible to us even independently of a systematic theological doctrine concerning Mary. From this we can now begin to consider what that means for her and for us. If we then have a clearer and more distinct idea of the blessed Virgin before the eyes of our soul, we shall be better Christians, or at least know better what we really ought to be. And then again we can honour her with greater faith, in a more genuine and sincere way, which in turn will be a blessing for ourselves. Amen.

THE IMMACULATE CONCEPTION

AFTER attempting to form a comprehensive idea of the blessed Virgin, we are now going on to elucidate the various individual truths of faith concerning her, beginning quite simply and straightforwardly with that prerogative of grace in Mary that is chronologically the first in her life. The theme of our reflections is, then, the beginning of the life of the Mother of God, which faith terms her Immaculate Conception.

Now though it would be appropriate for every Christian with at least some knowledge of what his catechism teaches, to know what the expression "Immaculate Conception" of the blessed Virgin means, nevertheless one keeps on coming across the most remarkable misunderstandings of this dogma of holy Church, voiced not only by non-Catholic Christians, but by Catholics. The Immaculate Conception is, first of all, quite different from the virginal conception of Jesus in the womb of the blessed Virgin. The Immaculate Conception of the blessed Virgin does not mean, either, that the physical coming into existence of Mary through generation by her parents was in any respect physically different from that of other human beings. So this dogma does not in any way imply that the coming into existence of a human being through the conjugal love of two human persons, in itself involves any defilement, so that in order to avoid this, Mary had to have a privilege in this respect. The dogma of the Immaculate Conception has nothing to do with all these misunderstandings.

What is the meaning of the Immaculate Conception, then? The Church's teaching that is expressed in these words, simply states that the most blessed virgin Mother of God was adorned by God with sanctifying grace from the first instant of her existence, in view of the merits of Jesus Christ her son, that is, on account of the redemption effected by her son. Consequently she never knew that state which we call original sin, and which consists precisely in the lack of grace in men caused in them by the sin of the first man at the beginning of human history. The Immaculate Conception of the blessed Virgin, therefore, consists simply in her having possessed the divine life of grace from the beginning of her existence, a life of grace that was given her (without her meriting it), by the prevenient grace of God, so that through this grace-filled beginning of her life, she might become the mother of the redeemer in the manner God had intended her to be for his own Son. For that reason she was enveloped from the beginning of her life in the redemptive and saving

43

love of God. Such is, quite simply, the content of this doctrine which Pius IX in 1854 solemnly defined as a truth of the Catholic faith.]

We must now ask ourselves a little more precisely and in detail what all this means, which we have just formulated in the somewhat scholastic terminology of theology. Firstly, this dogma indicates that the beginning of each spiritual being is important, and is laid down by God. God gives the beginning. He gives the beginning, in which the whole is already contained, despite all the freedom and individual responsibility and creativity of man, despite all that is unexpected and surprising. God traces the plan of life, in his wisdom and unfathomable love. We can never get behind the beginning set for us by God. Before we can begin with free decision to ask ourselves, how and in what light we are going to regard our life and shape it, we are already situated, with a quite definite, limiting starting-point, called into our life with a quite determinate initial position, by the omnipotent will of the holy God our creator, from which there is no appeal. We can protest from the start, sinfully, against this fixing of our starting point; we can give ourselves or refuse ourselves to God, within the framework of the possibilities determined for us by this starting point, but we are always inescapably dealing with what God has placed for us at our beginning.

Furthermore, the Immaculate Conception means that God surrounds the life of man with redemptive love. He dwells in awe-inspiring glory. There is no court to which one could appeal against him. One is absolutely at his mercy. We were not there when he traced the lines of our life. No one saw these plans before they were carried into effect. He who alone plans, God, is free, subject to none, independent, and in the majestic authority of his decision always in the right, whatever dispositions he makes for us. He can justly condemn us. He can mirror and reveal himself with the radiant, changeless, unquestionable validity of his Godhead, throughout all the harmonies and dissonancies of the cleavages, the diversity and self-contradictions of the created universe. He remains himself, though we stray, even if we are nothing, even if we were the lost. Only in a mute silence, more deathly than pure nothingness, can the creature, of itself, listen to that summons to come into existence, which of itself brings it before a court that has jurisdiction over life and death. We only know about that summons when it has been delivered, irrevocably. Even when it is for what is so much a consequence of our freedom that we cannot throw the responsibility on to God, even then that *fiat* issues from him who is the beginning and the end, unique, perfectly intelligible in himself but ever unfathomable to us. Since such is he, it is the most shattering fact, that we truly can and must declare this summons of the sovereign and incomprehensible God to be one of love, of genuine love that we can understand, to a court of grace, that it is creative of everlasting happiness, a miracle that does not condemn, but saves. We do not know with certainty that such a call as this is addressed to us, though we must firmly hope that it is. But it has already been uttered. That fact alone is rich in promise. For we can and must believe that such a call, comprising the whole of life from the beginning with saving mercy, was addressed to Mary. Everything of course proceeds from the unfathomable, mysterious depths of the eternal Godhead, which to God are radiant light, though to us impenetrable darkness. Yet something has arisen, emerged from the deep, ultimate, all-embracing will of the Godhead, where the Father in truth decides the lot of his own Logos. And to pay honour to the one transcendent Godhead, it is not a Vulcan's fire that falls over the empty fields of nothingness, but tender, holy joy, the gentleness of the Holy Spirit, light and life and kindness, mercy, consolation, and beauty unalloyed: a human being who from the beginning is good and encompassed by everlasting love. That is something we can understand, for it is what we ourselves should be, like our wistful daydreams of what a human being should be.

Now if that is true for one, it is true for all. Our God willed to love one human being in that way, but in that love of his for Mary, encompassing her whole life with love from beginning to end, we too are implied. For God loved Mary like that because he willed his Son to be a human being in a community of human beings, of which we are members, to be their redeemer, the real pledge and guarantee that his grace is more powerful than our guilt.

46

So the Immaculate Conception of the blessed Virgin reveals that God loves humanity as such. He formed the idea of man because he was thinking of his own self, because he formed the idea of himself existing also as a beloved human being in that created world distinct from himself where what is horrible can lodge, as a human being receiving his nature from another – from a mother – from one who is not God and yet gave God to himself.

The Immaculate Conception also means that God surrounds this life of humanity with loving fidelity. It means not only a holy, blessed beginning, not only the undefiled purity of a human being's origin, but a beginning that originates from God who is faithful. The beginning was what it was because the end was to be blessed. Such a beginning was made so that what came of it might become the source of God himself made man. The beginning was heavenly because loving omnipotence looked to the blissful end. This dogma affirms that God's gifts are without repentance. He is faithful; having given the beginning, he will bring it to its end, proclaims this truth of the faith. God's plans are made with the end in view, God always envisages the whole. That applies in the first place to Mary, to be sure. But the mere fact that it holds true at all of someone, is itself rich in promise for all. It is only because we are so dull and egotistical that we cannot understand that there is light for us if light is lit anywhere. That is the only reason why it is possible for us to think that not much is said for us, when this glorious thing is said to Mary. As soon as we no longer take up a distant, individualistic and egotistic attitude towards her, what is valid for her effectively extends its scope to us. We ourselves then become the blessed prisoners of God's fidelity, unable any more to escape from him; those whom he comes to meet on whatever road they may travel, because they always move into the limitless domains that are his. It is quite certainly a holy solace to realize that he was so faithful in the case of his handmaid, the mother of his Son, that the holy beginning of her life already included unfailingly its holy end, even though that end had to be won from that beginning, freely and responsibly.

The Immaculate Conception means that Mary possessed grace from the beginning. What does it signify, though, to say that someone has sanctifying grace? This dry technical term of theology makes it sound as though some *thing* were meant. Yet ultimately sanctifying grace and its possession do not signify any *thing,* not even merely some sublime, mysterious condition of our souls, lying beyond the world of our personal experience and only believed in a remote, theoretical way. Sanctifying grace, fundamentally, means God himself, his communications to created spirits, the gift which is God himself. Grace is light, love, receptive access of a human being's life as a spiritual person to the infinite expanses of the Godhead. Grace means freedom, strength, a pledge of eternal life, the predominant influence of the Holy Spirit in the depths of the soul, adoptive sonship and an eternal inheritance.

Mary does not differ from us because she possessed these gifts. It is her possession of them from the beginning, and incomparably, that is the sole difference between her and us. As for the content of this gift, its nature and intrinsic meaning, the eternal Father could not intend anything for the mother of his incarnate Son, without intending it for us too, and giving it to us in the sacrament of justification. For us too he eternally intended this saving grace from the beginning, in his eternity, even though it was only effected in us after the beginning of our earthly, temporal life, in order that it might be plain that it is all his grace, that nothing in our salvation belongs to us of ourselves. God has eternally kept his eternal love in readiness for us too, so that in the moment that we call our baptism, he may come into the depths of our heart. For we too are redeemed, saved, marked with God's indelible seal. We too have been made the holy temple of God. In us too the triune God dwells. We too are anointed, hallowed, filled with the light and life of God. We too have been sent by him, from this beginning, into our life, that we too may carry the light of faith and the flame of love through this world's darkness, to the place where we belong, in his eternal radiance, his eternity.

Are we so different, then, from her who was conceived immaculate? May we not say that God did not will this difference between us principally because he loved us less, and therefore did not give us the gift of grace, which is himself, from the beginning, but rather so that through this difference, the full range of significance of grace might find clear expression? In Mary and her Immaculate Conception it is manifest that eternal mercy from the beginning has enveloped man, and therefore us, children of Adam and Eve, sinners, and so it is clear that God does not leave us unaided. We who first come into existence graceless in soul, proclaim the truth that we are not the beloved children of God by our own powers, not by our intrinsic, inalienable nature, wide and noble though its capacity may be, but only by the sheer grace of God alone, which is given to us, the sinners, without any claim or any merits.

Finally, the Immaculate Conception shows that God's call is a summons to what is most individual. He establishes the beginning in love and irrevocable fidelity to his own plan, he lays down grace as the real and comprehensive beginning, for Mary and for us. But this plan is, precisely, one which plans that man shall be free, shall have a history, involving what man himself does, what he dares and achieves, what he suffers and what is his own. God does not diminish us, he gives us to ourselves. He disposes our life as something of which we ourselves have the disposal. He does not create statues, but men, who from the beginning that only he can give, can make and mould themselves. Only because he can make such creatures, did it please God to create. Otherwise he would have kept his ideas within his own mind and rejoiced in them only in his contemplation of his own inner life. But since he himself willed to savour, in the person of his Word, that

50

created freedom distinct from himself, he willed to utter his own Word as man and therefore free, into the world of finite things, and in consequence he willed a mother of his Son, who should give him the fruit of life from the tree of created being. And because he willed a mother, he willed her to be like his incarnate Logos himself, free in herself even before God. Consequently the first beginning of this mother is truly like the start of a real journey, where one has to find one's way. That is why the glorious beginning, rich in love and immutable irrevocable fidelity, was, nevertheless, the beginning of a life-story, an adventure, a beginning that gave rise to more than it actually contained. It was truly only a beginning precisely because it could do that; but it could only do so because it always remained profoundly receptive to the infinite vitality of God and could draw from him, and not merely from its limited intrinsic character as a beginning, things novel, fresh and unexpected, individual and unique. Such forward movement from a beginning is hard and incomprehensible, unfathomable like God himself, an image of his infinity. It is tears and tedium, distress and bitterness, agony and death, joy and light, courage and greatness, a whole long and always unprecedented human life. But it is something which – however incomprehensibly to the weary heart of man! – is eternally worthy to be, or rather it is eternity and God himself contemplates it through eternity and since he himself is of course involved in it, a whole eternity does not exhaust it.

51

May the blessed Virgin forgive us for having spoken more about man in general than about her alone. She was meant. We always know of God only what he tells us of himself by what he does. We always know him only by contemplating his works, but in them we see him as he wills to be in our regard. For however free and incalculable his separate works may be, they have meaning and connection and one work that he has brought about is a promise of what he will yet do. Since he did for Mary what the mystery of the Immaculate Conception tells us about her, we know that what he himself did by the Incarnation of his Logos overflows for mere humanity as love and fidelity, grace, divine life and the eternal value of each individual existence. With us, it is still an urgent matter of our becoming what we are, so that we may hear the summons that in grace has already been addressed to us, so that we may freely, by this grace, produce the end that corresponds to the beginning that God established. But we too are those who are called, who are enveloped from beginning to end by God's power, his love and his fidelity to us even in what is most individual and our own. May the blessed Virgin whose first beginning was holy and pure, pray for us, that we too may become what we are. Amen.

MARY THE MOTHER OF GOD

WE have reflected, in accordance with the Church's teaching, on the holy origin of the blessed Virgin. We recalled that, encompassed by the grace of God which marked her out in advance to be the mother of the redeemer, she was filled from the first with that divine life that we call sanctifying grace and was preserved from the sin which is transmitted to all of us from Adam. The Church's teaching has nothing to say about the course of her life from the moment her existence began until the day when the angel brought her the message from heaven. It remains a secret, in God's keeping, what the blessed Virgin did and suffered, with that origin and that grace as a basis, until the day when the angel greeted her. It will have been what was usual and ordinary, for human ostentation and God's grace do not go together. Mostly it is unconsciously taken for granted, and what God provides day by day life assimilates as though things could not be otherwise, and so God is served in faith and love absolutely unreservedly, and the ordinary everyday actually becomes the form that reveals the heavenly endowment.

53

So now we must consider that this holy virgin became the mother of Jesus Christ our Lord and saviour; the fact that Mary is the mother of God. As the reflection of the Church, guided by her faith, attained a more and more explicit awareness and expression of the divine sonship of our Lord and saviour Jesus, and of the unity of his divine person despite – and in – the duality of natures, human and divine, it was correspondingly certain from the first, in this belief and mind of the Church, that Mary the mother of Jesus, the mother of this God-man, is the mother of God. What the Church proclaimed with the words "born of the virgin Mary", as having been handed down from the beginning by the apostles, was solemnly defined at the Council of Ephesus in 431, by the notion of the divine motherhood, which had already become a tradition. To this day Christians of all denominations are called upon to confess their belief in the divine motherhood of the blessed Virgin, with the whole of tradition, and the reformers of the sixteenth century too. There can indeed be no question of genuine Christianity, truly believing in the coming of God himself in human flesh, if this oldest of the articles of faith concerning Mary is no longer held firm, or if an attempt is made shamefacedly to disregard it. It is clear that only very little can be said here about this mystery of the faith, which really implies the whole substance of Christian belief.

If we read Holy Scripture on the mystery we are now dealing with, it will strike us that it does not primarily tell us of the dignity of Mary by recounting the facts of her physical motherhood in regard to Jesus, though of course it does this, or tell us that Mary is the mother of God as a consequence of a physical event. It rather tells us directly what Mary did, and this shows her importance and her dignity. Luke does not envisage the greatness and importance of the blessed Virgin primarily from the viewpoint that she is the mother of God. He shows us the blessed Virgin becoming, through the consent of her obedience in faith, blessed among women. Of course this consent in faith derives its greatness and its significance in the divine plan of redemption from the fact to which it refers, the divine motherhood. But because this divine motherhood is described from the start not as a merely physical occurrence, but as taking place through a free, personal, grace-inspired act of faith, the whole mysterious event is at once singled out from a mere private destiny, a biographical relationship of Mary to Jesus, her son, and inserted into the history of faith and redemption. Thus Mary appears as a figure in sacred history, like Abraham and other characters in the historical dialogue between God and mankind, on whose right decision our salvation too depends, and on whom we are built up as on a foundation. We are told quite simply and plainly in Scripture: Look, there was a human being to whom an angel came with a mysterious message, and this human being said, simply and unreservedly: Be it done unto me according to thy word; and through these

55

words of the blessed Virgin the Son of the eternal Father came down to this earth, to our flesh, into our history, and God has assumed for ever this world, in the flesh of his Son. And all that happened because Mary, by the consent of her faith, became the mother of God. The way Holy Scripture tells of her divine motherhood, then, involves Mary at once and as a matter of course in the tremendous, mysterious, shatteringly great drama that is being acted out between the eternal God and this world with its one human race. If, therefore, we wish to grasp or at least to form some idea of what is meant when the faith says she is the mother of God, the mother of the incarnate Word of the eternal Father, we must never view this motherhood as a merely physical one, but see it as a free, personal act of her faith, within the context of sacred history. We must also reflect, too, what we are really saying, when we confess with faith, as we genuflect, that "the Word was made flesh".

God created the world, it is his handiwork. Therefore everything belongs to God, because everything in heaven and earth, everything that is not him, is the work of his almighty will and a faint expression of his eternal being. But this world of God's can either stand infinitely distant from him, or it can be drawn by him wholly into his own divine life. Which of the two possibilities, that alone give ultimate meaning to everything, is realized, is not finally decided by the fact of creation; it is not decipherable from below, from the world itself, but, as viewed from the world, is only decided in the course of history. God created a free world of persons, angels and men, and so a drama develops between God and the world. For God is not the only one who is active, himself producing the drama of world history as though it were performed by puppets. His incomprehensible omnipotence consists precisely in his being able to place his creature in a freedom which is really its own. So there actually does arise in the history of this world a tremendous dialogue between the free God and free man. And here is its specific character. Viewed from God's side, the dialogue is in itself always open. Man can act freely as long as his history lasts, he can choose again and again to take up, out of the finite possibilities offered by his freedom, a new attitude in response to God's action. But to anything man does from among his limited possibilities and to which he commits his freedom, God can answer in innumerable ways, for he always has the unlimited possibilities of his infinite freedom at his disposal. He can respond to the action of the creature as he wills, incomprehensibly and unfathomably, in ways that to us are incalculable. So we really do not know, from our side, how this infinite God will act in our regard. Even if we have experience of some action of God concerning us, no general principle can be drawn, on such a basis alone, that he must act in the same way even at the next moment of our life. How could we know on our own, whether it is his will to be for us a consuming judgement or immeasurable mercy?

57

Whether he will dismiss us, creatures that emerge from nothingness, infinitely far from himself, there to move as if in orbit, circling immeasurable distances around that remote primordial sun of reality, or whether it is his will to take his creature to his heart and share with him his innermost life? Viewed from the world, all that is really open and undecided. And even after a long experience by the world of its creator, the outcome and last word of this dialogue would of itself remain indeterminate, because the eternal God would have just as infinite a multitude of possibilities at his disposal as he had at the beginning. God would never need to say his last decisive word in that unending drama, that unceasing dialogue. He could go on finding new and surprising answers to whatever words of praise or accusation mankind found to cry to God over the abyss of nothingness.

But everything has been quite different. God has spoken his last, definitive, all-inclusive, absolutely irrevocable word. He has actually uttered it into the world, so that he cannot recall it any more, or give it a new interpretation through another utterance. He has said this word by uttering his eternal WORD, the complete expression of himself, into the midst of this world, so that he has become a part of the world itself, in the very flesh of humanity. An irrevocable fact has been created by God through the Word's remaining the Word of God and yet becoming a real part of the world. The eternal God has himself determined that the world itself shall definitively be drawn into his eternal mercy, and it now has a goal which infinitely transcends it and yet is its own: God's own self. When we genuflect and say: And the Word was made flesh, we are saying that judgement is not God's last word, but mercy; not infinite remoteness, but indescribable presence; not his searing holiness and inaccessibility, but ineffable love, in which he gives himself to what is not God.

But the Word was made flesh because a maiden of our race knelt down at the angel's message and in the freedom of her heart and with the total unconditional gift of herself said: Be it done unto me according to thy word. God willed this freely given love of his creature as the means by which the eternal Word of the Father should enter the world to take this world up into his own life. That was the way he willed to come into this world. As a consequence, Mary, of the same race as ourselves, is the portal of eternal mercy, the gate of heaven, through which we are in fact saved and redeemed and taken up into the life of God. Of course this freedom of the blessed Virgin, her obedient consent in faith, the acceptance of redemption and God's presence by the world in the person of Mary, was itself a grace bestowed by God because he willed to come. Even this obedience in faith, therefore, derives from the unfathomable decree of God's mercy, of which it is the effect, not the cause. It was the presupposition created by God in the freedom of his creature in preparation for his coming into the world. It remains free, but obediently subject to grace.

But though God in the free, spontaneous, autonomous sovereignty of his grace gives everything, even the blessed Virgin, even her love, her freedom, even the free consent itself, that does not mean that this consent which God prepared as a presupposition of his coming, was not the blessed Virgin's own consent. When God gives, when he gives his gifts, when he freely disposes of his gifts, these things become precisely what is most our own, precisely because it is he, the infinite and omnipotent, who gives them. And the higher the gift of God, and the more absolutely (to use human terms) it depends on him, the more it is our own property, because it is God-given. Nothing else that we are given by anyone, by nature or parents, outward circumstances, friends, chance, can become our own, intimately and personally, in any degree that compares with what the eternal God gives us in his holy grace. If he gives us something, it truly belongs to us; it truly constitutes the actual concrete reality of a human individual, not in spite of its being a grace of God, but precisely because it is one, purely and unfathomably, received simply from his freely bestowed mercy. When God willed the blessed Virgin through her free consent to her motherhood to open the world to the eternal mercy of God, this consent was in its very essence hers, her act. It belongs to her and cannot be taken from her. She is and remains for ever the person who for us and for our salvation and in this sense in our name, uttered that word of consent through which the Word of God was made flesh.

The divine motherhood of the blessed Virgin is therefore God's grace alone, and her own act, inseparably. It is not simply a physical motherhood, it is her grace and her deed, placing her whole self, body and soul, at the service of God and his redemptive mercy to mankind. And since this divine motherhood – as an act of faith personally made – belongs intrinsically to the history of redemption, it gives Mary a real relationship to us, for we are living in the history of redemption which she has decisively influenced. She has a place in our creed and our piety. When we praise her divine motherhood, we are not merely honouring a prerogative that belongs to her private life, deriving only from a physical event, and constituting a sort of juridical title of honour, which really concerns and has more to say about the union of two natures in the unity of the one person of the Word of God than about Mary herself. If we understand the divine motherhood of Mary in a comprehensive sense, that is, as comprising Mary's whole rôle and reality, and as belonging to the history of redemption, we also grasp at once that Mary is truly our mother. We understand our duty to call her blessed, with all the generations, because what we are blessing, the Son of her blessed womb, and her holy motherhood, is our salvation. We will always cry with Elizabeth: And whence is this to me, that the mother of my Lord should come to me? We will repeat the words: And blessed art thou that hast believed, because those things shall be accomplished that were spoken to thee by the

Lord. And we can add to that on our own account: Blessed are we because she has believed. And as we pray again and again: Holy Mary, mother of God, pray for us sinners, now and at the hour of our death, – we are making a profession of faith in the divine motherhood of the blessed Virgin, and we are confident of our own salvation, because she believed, and in faith, in body and soul and heart, and in her blessed womb, received Jesus Christ our Lord and our eternal salvation. Amen.

THE VIRGIN MARY

WE have tried to set out a few reflections on the divine motherhood of Jesus' holy mother. The creed handed down to us from a very early age of the Church, and known as the Apostles' creed, explicitly proclaims this belief in the divine motherhood of Mary in the words: *ex Maria virgine,* born of the virgin Mary. Since the earliest days of the Church, and as Luke's account shows, since the time of the apostles, it has therefore been the express belief of the Church that Mary was a virgin even as a mother. The Church has consequently always taught as part of its belief, and defended against false doctrines, that Mary conceived her son without the co-operation of an earthly father and remained a virgin after the birth of Jesus too. We need say no more about the direct meaning of this doctrine of faith, for it is clear from the words themselves. At most it may seem necessary to say something about what we mean when it is said that the Virgin Mary was not only a virgin before and after the birth of our Lord, but also in his birth. It is not easy to give the exact significance

of this expression of very ancient tradition, which refers
to an item of authentic doctrine. We can perhaps make
clear what is meant as follows. There are physical events
which, however naturally they may appear to be the
direct consequences of the constitution of man, yet must
be recognized by the more penetrating and comprehensive eye of faith, which sees man as a being called to a
supernatural life and a divine end, as being in fact the
consequences of original sin, at least in the form in which
they actually occur in this or that human being. Death for
example, pain and suffering, the blindly impersonal desires
of our bodily nature, and likewise, according to the testimony of Scripture (Gen. 3:16), some accompaniments of
motherhood. We cannot say without further ado that
Mary was simply spared everything that with us is a
consequence and outward expression of our origin in
original sin, because she was sinless and conceived immaculate. For of course she had in the highest degree a share in
the lot of her Son, our redeemer, who became our saviour
precisely by suffering to the end the sin of the world, in
the pain, darkness and death, which are sin's bodily results.
It is for that reason of course that we honour Mary too as
the Mother of Sorrows. But since Mary, as we have still
to consider, is sinless, and, being free from concupiscence,
could fit the burden of a life of sorrows into the activity
of her faith and love in a way quite different from us in
our frailty, the process of her motherhood could not take
place in exactly the same way as in a human being subject

to concupiscence as a consequence of original sin. Though it is difficult to say more precisely what that meant in actual fact, and as it is perhaps better not to try to define this special character of the blessed Virgin's child-bearing, nevertheless one can to some extent perceive from such considerations as these, that the motherhood of Mary, corresponding to her person and her sinlessness, must have been different in various respects. That may be sufficient to justify our speaking of her virginity in child-birth.

Though the doctrine of the perpetual virginity of Mary requires no long explanation in itself, nevertheless a Christian's faith imposes on him the task of reflecting on its significance. Why should God dispose his grace in regard to this human being in such a way that he willed her to remain ever a virgin? After all, that is not really a matter of course. Only someone who does not realize the high dignity of pure married love could think it goes without saying that this would have been unbecoming in the mother of the Lord. There is, therefore, no sense in first of all taking for granted virginity consecrated to God as an ideal in itself, and on that principle praising the Virgin Mary as an ideal example of such virginity. Such a procedure makes it difficult to avoid the danger of disparaging the meaning and importance of matrimony and married love, and especially for a Christian, of forgetting that matrimony, married love and fertility are consecrated by one of Christ's sacraments.

If we are to understand the reason for the virginity of the holy mother of God, and then (and only then), try to understand what Christian virginity really is, we must first note that in Holy Scripture this virginity of the mother of God is always mentioned in connection with her dignity as mother of God. Scripture in fact only knows of Mary as both virgin and mother of God. We can leave the question for the moment whether the grace of divine motherhood formed and shaped the blessed Virgin, without her explicitly realizing it, throughout her life from the beginning, so that her intention to remain a virgin had already been formed before the message of the angel, or whether virginity only became consciously willed at the moment of the angel's message, on account of her vocation and function as mother of the Messiah. We can do so because in any case she possessed the whole dignity of the will to virginity, in the unconditional surrender of her entire self in obedience and faith to the will of God, even if within the mental perspectives of the Old Testament, she may not, we may suppose, have explicitly realized before the angel's message, that this will of God, to which she was entirely submissive, signified for her perpetual virginity. At all events it is clear that with her this grace of virginity is a radiation from within outwards, a consequence of her vocation to divine motherhood, a factor intrinsic to this principal function and dignity of hers, and must be understood in that light. Her will to virginity is in a true sense fully comprised in the readiness of the blessed Virgin to submit absolutely and unreservedly always and everywhere to the decrees of God's holy will, in whatever form; it was implicit in her freedom and her love as she said: Behold the handmaid of the Lord.

Consequently, if we must think of Mary's virginity from the point of view of her divine motherhood and her willing consent to it, the question of the meaning of this virginity changes to the question: Why did the Son of God, the eternal Word, will to become man without having an earthly father? It may perhaps sound surprising, but we cannot simply answer: Because the Son of God had a Father in heaven. For the fact that this man born of Mary is the Son of the eternal Father, is not due to this man Jesus having no earthly father; it is because the eternal Word, who is the Son of God the Father, assumes a human nature, and consequently has a Father in heaven because of his divine personality as Son, whatever the origin of his human nature may in fact have been or might have been. If, therefore, the Son of God willed to become man, without having an earthly father, that is not because he has a father in heaven, but for some other reason. This reason is not as hard to understand as it may at first appear.

The Incarnation of the Son of God is grace absolutely, grace which can nevermore be removed from the course of the world, but which nothing in the history of the world presupposes, nor anything in the natural constitution of things. The actual realization of the incarnation of the Son of God is the absolutely free and incalculable mystery

67

of divine grace, and as such, stems not from below but entirely from above. The world and its conditions and claims and intrinsic potentialities offers from below no compelling reason why the eternal God himself should descend into its history. Since, therefore, in this sense, the Son of God did not come of the will of man or of the will of the flesh, from the world's forces and energies, he correspondingly willed to become man in such a way that it would be clear from the very manner of his coming that his origin is not of this earth, from the inner forces of this world, not even from the noblest and holiest human love, but wholly from on high. For that reason the incarnate Son of God willed to have no earthly father, so that it might be plain in the clearest fashion that he came wholly by God's decree and not from the world. He did not will it so, as if the world were evil or marriage not an institution of his own founding, nor as if the normal, natural coming into existence of a human being were in some way tainted with a dubious slur, but simply and solely so that it might be made plain to all that the earthly fabric of things, even of the noblest weave, is here interrupted. Vertically downwards came the incalculable mercy of God, the incarnation of the Son, and though he takes from our flesh and our race the nature he wills to assume, yet in his humanity he was entirely the effect of the free action of the eternal God on high.

Mary placed herself at the disposal of this action of God, so totally that in her the gift of God in person, God made man, could appear, truly of us and yet wholly from on high. Because he is not of this world, but from on high, Mary is the Virgin. In her it is made plain and manifest that there is something beyond the powers and forces of this world, even the noblest, the most important, those that serve to increase humanity, to found nations and produce human life; something that transcends them and is beyond their scope, which is grace, and occurs only by the favour of the eternal God. Her virginity, and the origin of our Lord without an earthly father, signify one and the same thing, not in words, but in easily understood terms of human life: God is the God of freely bestowed grace, who cannot be drawn down from on high by all our endeavours, whom we can only receive as the inexpressibly freely given gift of himself. Mary was not only called to live that, in heart and mind, but visibly to represent and proclaim it by all she was, even in her physical existence. That is why she is a virgin spiritually and physically, solely and entirely at God's disposal.

Because her whole existence, all that she was throughout her life, from her conception to her death, was totally absorbed into this function of being the mother of God; because apart from it she is nothing; because she had no other purpose; because in everything she was, with all her powers, and in every situation in life, she was dedicated to this one vocation; because of all this, she was ever a virgin, ever and always by reason of her divine motherhood as the obedient acceptance of grace. And not only before

69

the conception of her divine Son, but also ever afterwards. For then too she was and remained still the same, total receptivity to the free gift of grace from on high. She was not only to be that, but also to represent it for the Church as an exemplar actively inspiring imitation, and so found in the Church virginity as a state of life. She has no other function in this world but one, to receive, not earthly powers for earthly life, but divine grace alone, not only in her mind and heart, though that was the most important, but also in her visible and tangible earthly existence.

Now has all this anything to do with us, or is it in every respect a privilege that belongs only to divine motherhood, the radiance and consequence of that supreme vocation and dignity, something which, because it is unique, has no relevance for us? On the contrary, Mary has become a model of all Christian virginity. It is not by chance that in sacred history virginity consecrated to God has only existed since the blessed Virgin. But she is not only a model and sanction for those who, for the sake of the kingdom of God and in accordance with our Lord's counsel, for love of God and the service of the Church, renounce the great blessing of matrimony. Mary's virginity has an important message for all Christians. In the first place this attitude of expectation, of readiness and receptivity to grace from on high, this awareness that the ultimate thing is grace and grace alone, is something which, as an attitude of mind, every Christian must have, even if it does not find concrete expression in virginity in the strict sense as a visible and organized state of life in the Church. For ultimately none of us work out our salvation by our own power. We do not gain heaven simply and solely by vindicating this earth. We are not building towers of Babel, in which man and his powers and potentialities gradually mount up till they reach heaven. After we have used all the forces the earth offers and have done our utmost, we are once again the indigent beggars and unprofitable servants who must receive what really and finally matters from God and from him alone. And we are only really Christians when we do approach God with this virginal attitude of mind, which, to be sure, may appear to the world to be sterile. Ultimately it is only in such a way that rightfully, in accordance with God's will, and indeed blessed with his grace, we can receive and take into our lives with gratitude, marriage and conjugal love.

Each Christian must, therefore, somewhere and somehow in his life live through, undergo, what corresponds to this virginal attitude of the blessed Virgin. That is the second point. The Christian is not only to imitate something of this virginal attitude of Mary merely in his attitude of mind. Even those who are married must somehow, in the actual exterior details of life repeat what in Mary's whole life is made manifest with the clarity that belongs to her as representative and exemplar, that is to say, an ability to renounce good things of this world, not only where the world is sinful, base and in darkness, but also where it is fair and precious and joyous; an ability to renounce because one really and actually believes, not merely as an abstract and reasonable theory, that all that is not God's grace from on high is secondary and in the final resort insignificant. That certainly does not mean that the Christian must pass by all fair and precious earthly things, but the Christian is not truly a Christian, if he has not the courage now and again, when the world is beautiful and strong, full of life and excitement, to pass by, as a sign that the Christian, like Mary, receives what is unlooked for, and redemption is precisely that, purely as a grace from on high. Because grace comes from heaven, the blessed Virgin exists, and consequently virginity in the Church, and so in every Christian life the attitude of mind put into practice, of receiving grace from on high with the real faith that expresses itself in the sacrifice of something good and holy in the world. Amen.

MARY WITHOUT SIN

BEYOND what is contained in Scripture, the Church knows nothing of the life of the blessed Virgin or the external events of which it was made up. No historically trustworthy tradition that might add to Scripture has been preserved in the Church. It is as if all these details were really fundamentally unimportant, and were hidden in God's mystery, so that men might only know the one thing that matters, that is, that Mary is the mother of the Lord. For all that, the Church's faith concerning Mary does give a comprehensive knowledge and one that expresses what is decisive in the details of her life, not only concerning the great moment when she received the message of the angel and conceived the Word of the eternal Father for the salvation of the world, but also about what really sums up Mary's whole life. The Church knows that Mary was always sinless, was preserved not only from original sin, but also completely and perpetually preserved from every personal sin. That was expressly affirmed in 1546 by the Council of Trent, to be the Church's belief.

This might at first seem surprising, and if as a result we inquire into the history of this doctrine, we find that in the early Church there were one or two ecclesiastical writers in the first centuries who had doubts about this truth or, as though dazzled by it, were not able to bear its full radiance. So it is not strange if we are at first rather astonished at this doctrine of the faith. We might ask, surely man is sinful? Doesn't it belong to him to be weak and frail and inadequate, ever needing to have recourse to the forgiving mercy of God? If he does not understand that he is a sinner, isn't he still not in that truth, which God wills to reveal to him, in order to deliver him? Isn't it written that man is a liar? That "If we say that we have no sin, we deceive ourselves, and the truth is not in us" (1 John 1: 8). And doesn't it belong to the truth of man, to his genuineness, to the clear grasp he must have of his own situation, if he is to work out his salvation, that he must trust absolutely and solely to the eternal, unmerited, incalculable mercy of the God of grace? How can that person who, after Christ, pre-eminently and in the truest sense deserves the name of human being, be an exception to this truth?

Furthermore, Mary is after all redeemed; and precisely because she is the mother of her own redeemer, does not wish to have anything that she does not owe to him. She has received all she is from the abyss of grace of the eternal Father, who has taken her lovingly to be his daughter and out of pure grace has made her the mother of his Son and the temple of the Holy Spirit. Mary is she who is redeemed and totally redeemed, and who wills to be nothing except total receptivity, by the grace of the Lord. Can she, therefore, be perfectly sinless?

This question is to be met with another. Is one less redeemed, if one has not sinned? Does one need God's mercies more in receiving forgiveness of sins, or if one receives grace not to sin at all? If we are to answer this question, we shall have to say that the freedom from sin of a human being in this world, living in the darkness of this world, is more grace, more redemption, than when a human being is taken up out of the darkness he has loved, into God's light. To be preserved from sin is a more splendid, radiant redemption, but still redemption pure and simple. One who is preserved from sin does not after all save himself, does not give himself this freedom from sin by his own power. All righteousness is God's gratuitous gift and all perseverance in it is again a grace which no human being can merit. The favour that is bestowed in the forgiveness of sin does not consist in a human being's having fallen into sin, – that is the person's own fault alone, and gives him no right to pardon, and in itself has no intelligible significance, – but consists in the person's being given the grace of justification. But this is the purely gratuitous gift that is made to one who remains preserved from sin.

So when we say that, in the belief of the Church, and in accordance with the testimony of Holy Scripture, God's redemption through Jesus Christ has been realized in Mary in its most splendid, perfect and comprehensive way,

75

and has been manifested in sacred history through her divine motherhood, we must as a consequence acknowledge that Mary must be the sinless virgin, full of grace, mother of God. For that we do not need to know the details of her life. The Church has no need to carry out a laborious process of canonization in order to determine whether it is true that Mary practised in a heroic manner throughout life the virtues that God's grace give the true Christian. The Church only needs to know one thing, that her redemption was perfect, occurred utterly and triumphantly. Then the Church cannot profess this except by saying that Mary was sinless throughout her life. And the Church must proclaim this, because she must acknowledge herself to be the historically manifest arrival of the triumphant grace of God in the Last Days, which dawned with the Resurrection. For the Church is not, of course, merely the messenger bearing God's commands and a mere offer of grace, of which no one ever knows anywhere, whether in fact it wins the victory in the free consent of men. The Church is the tangible presence, in the sacred history of redemption, of the victory of grace, the community of those truly redeemed, Holy Church. She cannot, of course, say this with certainty of each of her members while she is still on her pilgrim journey far from the Lord; she has dead members too, and bears the scars of her bitter, sorrowful history of wanderings through this dark epoch on earth. But nevertheless, if she is to be Holy Church, indestructibly holy, because she is the Church of the Messianic age, not like the Synagogue, which could fall entirely from the grace of God; if she is to be holy in an actual and tangible manner, not only by propounding an abstract postulate, but as a sign set by God among the nations, claiming faith and supplying its ground, then the Church must be able to point with quite unambiguous certainty at least to some of her members and be able to say: Here in these I was Holy Church, and as such, have given testimony in these, that the grace of God in Jesus Christ is not merely a vague promise but victorious power. If this is so, as happens in the canonization of saints as part of the Church's pastoral office, then it is most certainly possible to the Church in regard to the holy mother of God. It must be possible here in a quite special, a unique way, for, of course, the origin of such knowledge here is not simply the moral impression (of a purely empirical kind), of the life of a holy person as a whole, and a few miracles, or martyrdom, but a truth of faith, namely, the divine motherhood understood in its full sense, as has been already explained, one of the central truths that the Church has to preach. Consequently the Church must be able to say at least once, that redemption by the grace of God produced its complete effect, and in such a way that this perfect victory becomes plainly manifest for us pilgrims, as a promise to us that "God does not give the Spirit by measure" (John 3: 34).

The Church knows that in this praise of Mary's sinlessness, she is not ascribing to Mary an excellence which she acquired by her own power, and which would give

77

her rights in relation to God. The Church is only praising in this way the pure and dazzling mercy of God.

From this standpoint we must once again glance into the life of the blessed Virgin, as far as the few slight details recorded here and there in Scripture permit. For in fact something remarkably surprising but also consoling emerges for us. One or two Fathers of the Church took offence at certain things narrated there about the life of the blessed Virgin, and said they were difficult to reconcile with her sinlessness. They were certainly wrong, and did not see as clearly and accurately as the Church, filled with love and enlightened by the Holy Spirit. Nevertheless, they felt something that is true, and that we ought to see more plainly today, because it is easily overlooked by too abstract a way of thinking about moral questions. The fact is, we often think holiness and absence of sin incompatible with ordinary life on this solid earth, where people laugh and cry, are born and die. We think holiness, when it actually exists, must take a "heavenly", ethereal form, or at least can only prosper far removed from the sturdy everyday world of the ordinary human being, perhaps behind the walls of a cloister. The holy life of the blessed Virgin, however, is startlingly like our own. She lived what, viewed from the outside, was a really commonplace and obscure life, enduring the ordinary petty round of any average woman in any odd corner of a small country, far from the great stream of history, of civilization and of politics. She set off on a search, she felt anxious, she did not know everything either, wept, had to ask her way and seek her way from stage to stage of her life's journey, like other human beings. She had to say to her divine Son: "Son, why hast thou done so to us? Behold, thy father and I have sought thee, sorrowing!" It is twice said of her that she did not understand what was said to her (Luke 2 : 33; 50). She first had to take a lot of things silently into her heart, keep them there, accepting their validity, so that later they might bear fruit in insight and understanding acceptance. She could only say: "Whatsoever he shall say to you, do ye", without knowing beforehand what he would do. She had to hear it said to her: "Woman, what is that to me and to thee?" (John 2 : 4). And when as his mother she wanted to get to her Son: "Who is my mother and my brethren? ... Whosoever shall do the will of God, he is my brother and my sister and my mother" (Mark 3 : 33–35). She stood under the cross of her Son. She played no striking part in the Church of the apostles. Certainly she is there, the mother of the Lord, in the midst of the original community praying for the coming of the Holy Spirit (Acts 1: 14), but she appears so unexceptional and ordinary to those around her, that she is only mentioned along with the other women and Jesus' relations. Perspective was needed to perceive the glory and the grace of God she must have had. It is clear that John, though he lived with her a long time, as our Lord had wished, was not yet very interested in biographical details of Mary's life. Luke who at the same time though with greater historical perspective, collected sources of information, showed greater interest in the account handed down here and there in pious circles about Mary, and Jesus' childhood. The Church similarly had to meditate for hundreds of years longer about Mary's life until it was finally possible to say, with the explicitness achieved by reaching full awareness of her belief: Behold, she is wholly fair, wholly without sin. Time was needed before the Church could utter her jubilant cry of faith with joyful heart. At last, a human being on this earth, an authentic, real human being, not an imaginary character in a novel, not the mere postulate of an ideal system of ethics, but a person of flesh and blood, with tears, toil, poverty, obscurity, but who is, wholly and utterly, purity, kindness, love, faithfulness, patience, compassion, and belongs to God alone, to such a degree that she "merited" – as the Church goes so far as to say – to become the mother of the Redeemer, even though this "merit" is a pure grace of God, the first grace that was imparted to her, and could not crown any previous merit. Yet all this splendour was confined and hidden in the sober, unassuming, ordinary ways of a human being such as we know only too well, and suffer from.

We must take sin seriously, and heed what Scripture says: Man is a liar. We must strive to ask ourselves repeatedly, whether our conscience too has not already become mendacious, whether God's standards have not already become so dim to us, that we no longer notice what sinners we are. We must repeatedly pray: Deliver me too from my hidden sins. Give me a clear mind and courage to testify against myself on behalf of your holiness, so that I may recognize I am a sinner, so that I may not deceive my own self about my own sins, with the falsehood of this world.

But precisely because we wish truly to stand in God's truth and not just in our own, what we have been considering about Mary should give us the courage to say: Everything in me after all cannot be so perverse and evil, recalcitrant to the grace of God, as it sometimes seems. A good deal in our virtues may only be appearance that hides evil; but a lot of what is apparently evil and imperfect on the surface, may only be the appearance that hides what God's grace in fact has triumphantly accomplished in us. In this life of darkness, weakness, poverty, ignorance, weariness and grief, one can after all be a human being who loves God and is loved by him, a child of God, living the life of the Spirit, sustained, enveloped and inescapably surrounded by the mercy of God. If we look to God and trust more to him and his testimony concerning his grace, than to what God the judge says of us and our wretchedness – and we may do so! – then we may also believe that our life and our weakness are really already so moulded by grace, that in the very depths of our being there dwells, not the evil spirit of darkness, but the radiant light of God; and we may trust that we too are on our way to God, and that our life is already such that it will end in blessedness.

Is that such a matter of course? It would be, if we were to suppose that the "good Lord" (as we call him, with an affectionate name that we are perhaps easily inclined presumptuously to misunderstand), must take it for granted that we should organize life as we think fit, or that he is really the one to apologize to us for the inadequacies of this life. Perhaps it would be a matter of course then! But since we know that God is the thrice holy, that with devouring and exclusive love he wants our whole heart, all our powers, our whole soul, in a single-minded love that draws everything into it, we must in truth ask ourselves in fear: Are we anything but wretched lost sinners who, through cowardly self-pity, are not willing to recognize this, and prefer to blame God's providence rather than our sins? If then we look at Mary, refuge of sinners, we must indeed say that she was the only entirely sinless person in the world. But her life, poor, insignificant, modest, sorrowful, gives us solace after all, and the strong hope that we are more than merely sinners, that God's grace is doing in us what it did in her; that we too are blessed by grace, and beloved; that we are, after all, faithful at heart, through God's mercy, not our own powers, that we are those who will endure to the end, although they don't know how they will still have strength next day to meet the demands of life and the tremendous demand of God, those who throughout such a life of darkness, love God as the blessed Virgin did, until it becomes finally manifest what we already are. And then it can be said of us too, that the thrice blessed and thrice holy God delivered us into his own sinlessness and holiness. Amen.

82

ASSUMED INTO HEAVEN

In a certain sense holy Church knows very little about the blessed Virgin. In the early centuries, no concern was shown for what in any serious sense might be called a biography of Mary. No picture of her exists, and apart from one or two small touches in the New Testament, no incidents of her life are known. In fact the Church does not know Mary's life-story, but does know what must be said about Mary in confessing the faith and praising the grace of God. And to this there belongs the origin given by God in his grace to Mary; her perpetual virginity as enduring self-abandonment to the disposition of God's providence alone; her sinlessness as the fruit of the perfect redemption that was accomplished in her; and her divine motherhood. To it there belongs also her holy end and consummation. About this the Church really does not need to know anything from history, except that Mary, as the mother of the Lord, is the most perfect fruit and work of his redemption. The Church does not know about this ending as if it were the last chapter of a set of narratives handed down in history concerning the life of the blessed Virgin. The Church recognizes the nature of this consummation as an intrinsic element in what she is told by her faith in the mother of God as such. This faith, in its turn, is an intrinsic element of the belief of the Church in the triumphant accomplishment of redemptive grace in the Church. Consequently, the Church, guided by the Holy Spirit, could leave time until she had thoroughly pondered and fully surveyed this mystery of faith concerning the blessed Virgin in all its bearings. The Church could allow herself centuries, because she allows herself to be guided by the Spirit of God, which is operative through all the centuries of the history of the Church, and because she follows that Spirit, and not the wit of men. Then as a consequence of allowing herself to be led by that Spirit, and of her having the superhuman courage to believe that that Spirit is always with her and is ever active with power in the ever renewed understanding of the unchanged revelation of Jesus Christ, the Church knows that she is not led and determined by theological subtleties and merely human wishes and longings, but by the infallible Spirit of God, which leads her into the depths of the one, ever identical and yet never ossified revelation of our Lord, and unfolds this revelation more and more before the believing mind of the Church.

So it is that since the Feast of All Saints, 1950, we finally know, after fifteen hundred years of perpetual growth in the Church's awareness of her belief, through the infallible definition of the Roman pontiff, that the immaculate virgin mother of God, after completing her earthly course, was assumed body and soul into heavenly glory. Even though the definition of the Pope, in his teaching capacity, has given every Christian supreme certainty that this truth belongs to the content of the divine and apostolic revelation that is committed to the keeping and progressive exposition of the Church, one cannot really say that, in content, this truth, which has now become a defined dogma, is new to the Church's consciousness of her belief. Not only has this truth been taught and believed undisputedly for centuries in the Church; not only had the question of the precise character of Mary's consummation been expressed some fifteen hundred years ago and answered in the sense of the present dogma, with increasing firmness, despite some hesitation and opposition at first; but anyone who really has the Catholic belief in the dignity of the mother of God, her importance in the history of redemption, her sinless holiness, her rôle as exemplar and type of the perfection of redemption as such, has at least by implication, in such belief, a knowledge of the perfect consummation which the present dogma expressly formulates, even if such a believer had not yet succeeded, or without the help of the Church would not have succeeded, in drawing out this content of what is believed. That there has been a growth in the degree of certainty of this truth of the faith is in accordance with the nature of the case, and can be observed in many other instances, even in doctrines of faith recognized by non-Catholic Christians as indispensable constituents of their belief as Christians.

It is not really surprising that the Church knows this truth concerning Mary's holy ending, and has found her way by this belief of hers to final certainty. For if the content of Mary's life is known, something can be said about the outcome and fruit of that life. The Church knows Mary's true identity, how she lived, what her importance in the divine plan of redemption was, and the part she played in the one great drama of sacred history. The Church knows how far advanced this one history of mankind is already, into the Last Days, in fact, that have come upon us since the Resurrection of our Lord (1 Cor. 10:11). For that reason the Church can already also say that Mary, with the whole reality of her life – with body and soul, therefore, – has entered into that perfect fulfilment which every Christian hopes for from the grace of God, as the one outcome and fruit of his own human life.

A human being is a unity. He consists, to be sure, of a body and a soul, but he isn't composed in such a way that their assemblage is merely a fortuitous accident for the constituent parts. From the beginning, in the creative design of God, he is a unity, by the one actual reality of his humanity and the unity of his last end and purpose. For that reason, he is only really complete and perfect, when he has received his one total fulfilment with the whole of his spiritual and corporeal nature. Ultimately, it is not possible to separate man into a soul that finds its perfection and consummation with God, and a body that is either left behind somewhere or in the end is adventitiously included in the already total felicity of the soul. On the contrary, the one human being, in his unity, is only really quite complete and perfected, when he is so, in the one concrete physical reality that constitutes him a man. That is precisely why the Church always spoke in her original preaching in ancient times, of the resurrection of the flesh, when the consummation of the whole human being was meant. By "flesh", the one, complete, true physical human being was meant, and of him the Church says that his last end and his perfection consists in sharing one day the eternal glory of his creator, with the entire reality that constitutes him, glorified in his body, surrounded by a new heaven and a new earth, filled in all his spiritual powers by the whole splendour of the eternal Word. That is the one eternal goal of man. The fact that it is not reached all at once, that it is achieved in a process of becoming, a development, by stages, is not really surprising, considering the mutable and progressive character of finite creatures, but does not alter the fact that a human being in his one total self only finds his total perfection and fulfilment when, with body and soul, he enters into heavenly glory. We cannot perhaps imagine this glory. We always find ourselves in difficulties if we try to say in detail what it means for man to reach perfection and completion in soul and body. But it would indeed be something to be wondered at, if human beings, for the moment quite enclosed within the bounds of time and space, could, out of their personal experience of this world, build up an accurate representation of what, as the glorious fulfilment of their life, awaits them, as the gift of the omnipotent and eternal God. If we could picture it, without falling into contradictions and inadequacies, it would not really be perfection. Both as spiritual persons and because we have been endowed by God with grace, we are infinite in our aspirations, and as a consequence we can recognize by our reason instructed and enlightened by faith, that God alone can be our last end, that only in him can we find satisfaction. But if we try to picture in detail what this endless perfection would be like, our imagination capitulates. But that is exactly what characterizes a pilgrim's knowledge of his goal, when he is making for his destination from infinitely far away. Nevertheless we can listen to God's message with faith: Man is called to enter with body and soul into God's life and God's own glory.

Now the whole history of salvation of the one human race is a single tremendous drama. We have already said that by the coming of the Word of God into the world, this sacred history has already entered its final phase, that a factor has already been established in this history which – though the lot of the individual may still be undecided – stamps it in its totality with the mark of finality. For the decisive truth of Christian faith is that the Lord is truly risen. And since it is in our humanity, in our flesh and blood, that he has risen, been glorified and taken up into the glory of his Father, that fundamental doctrine of Christianity proclaims from the start, that eternal glory is even now a possibility in the history of this world, this humanity and this flesh; already a possibility because in the flesh of Christ, which is a part of this world, it is already a reality.

Now faith tells us that Mary is the perfect achievement and work of redemption, and that this perfection of her grace has entered its final stage, because she has left this earthly life of space and time, and entered the phase of her life in which no new events take place in freedom as on earth, but the harvest sown within the confines of time is gathered into God's eternity. Mary, however, in her life on this earth was the highest, unmatched realization of redemption in a human being endowed with grace, as mother of God and consequently as the perfect type or representative of redemption in its very essence. And she has already attained her perfect beatitude – no one can doubt this, who believes that she, sinless and full of grace, has accomplished her earthly course. Furthermore, in the chronology of sacred history the hour is already far advanced, so that in principle, perfect attainment of perfection and beatitude in soul and body is already possible – this cannot be doubted either, by anyone who believes that Christ is risen with his human nature. Consequently, faith, coming to full awareness of its own content, cannot

89

but confess what the Church defined: After the completion of her earthly life, Mary was assumed body and soul into the glory of heaven.

What is the importance of this mystery of the faith for us? First of all it means that if we want to express the perfect accomplishment of Mary's glory, we can only say of her what we proclaim as our own hope for ourselves: the resurrection of the flesh and life everlasting. In that we have acknowledged her perfect beatitude. And by affirming of her what we hope for ourselves, because it is impossible to announce anything more glorious, even about her, we in fact praise the boundless greatness of the supreme eternal glory which is to be ours, and in this praise, the greatness of each human being as fashioned by the merciful grace of God.

Moreover, do we not live in an age in which man is intensively, almost mysteriously occupied with himself, not simply as a mind open to the endless expanses of knowledge and "progress", but with himself as flesh and blood, as corporeal, of the earth, physical, finite and mortal, seeing himself as hopelessly immured in his physical nature, in his inherited dispositions, in determining economic conditions? Don't some make an idol of this flesh, this physical humanity, whereas others hate it? Don't they all suffer by it? Isn't it unspeakably tortured, desecrated, tormented, and at the same time abused with scandalous absence of restraint? To this world of hated, idolized and suffering human flesh and blood, the Church announces her doctrine of the Assumption of the blessed Virgin body and soul into heaven. The Church does not preach merely schemes, principles, and abstract truths. She preaches facts of the power and everlasting mercy of God, facts that have already happened, in us mere mortal men, not only in Christ, the author of salvation, but in those who need redemption, who can take nothing for themselves but must receive everything that truly belongs to salvation and is not merely secular futility. The Church proclaims in this truth concerning Mary, that the flesh is saved. The flesh is already saved. The beginning has already been made, in a woman, a human being of our race, who has wept, suffered and died like the rest. The poor flesh that some hate and others worship, is already judged worthy to be eternally with God, eternally saved and acknowledged. Not only in the Son of the Father, who comes "from above", but in one of our race who, like us, was from "here below". The human situation in its concrete physical reality here and now, the theme of all present-day philosophy concerning man, is neither a wall that separates us for ever from God and eternally makes us "men without God", nor something that must be abolished, though indeed it must be transformed, in order to reach God himself. Rather was the flesh created by the Father on high, redeemed by the Son, made holy by the Spirit, and it is already saved for ever. In the midst of the anguish and distress of this generation, the Church, so readily accused of being political and attached to

91

earthly power, of liking to install herself far too positively in this world, of being insufficiently eschatological, raises her head and by proclaiming this doctrine of the faith, gazes towards the only hope in which she really trusts, the future of God, who is so far advanced with his Kingdom, that he has already begun to be wholly present. The Church looks on high and greets in Mary her own type and model, her own future in the resurrection of the body. Amen.

MEDIATRIX OF GRACES

UNTIL now we have tried to consider, from the point of view of the Church's teaching, how Mary really belongs to the faith we profess, and what the total picture is, that faith forms of her. We have reflected on her holy origin, her divine motherhood, her sinlessness; we have pondered her holy ending, her assumption into heaven. One might now ask, whether there is really anything to add? Have we not already mentioned, in one form or another, everything concerning Mary? Yes and No, might be the answer. Certainly everything has been referred to, in one way or another, yet everything can be summed up once more, at the end of these theological meditations, by asking ourselves, what does all this mean for us? Until now we have considered rather what Mary is in herself, for herself. Consequently we can bring these reflections to an end by examining what she really is for us.

This can be expressed in a phrase that is already in customary use in the Church, though it does not embody a defined truth in the strict sense. We can simply say that

Mary is our mediatrix. After all we have often prayed to our Lady as our advocate, our intercessor. We may indeed consider that the thesis concerning Mary as mediatrix is not yet a definite doctrine. Yet, if we remind ourselves that what we repeat in the Apostles' creed, is an unquestionable truth of faith, and that we there profess belief in the communion of saints; if we tell ourselves that there is veneration and invocation of saints, and intercession of the saints for us, on our behalf, in the holy community of God and his saints, then the doctrine of the mediation of the most blessed Virgin is already also quite familiar to us, in our awareness of what we believe.

Yet a grave objection might be raised, all the same, from the start, against the term mediation, and the thought that lies behind it, and the implied reality. One might say: Isn't Jesus Christ our Lord the mediator, the only mediator, between God and ourselves? And to this question, propounded in this form, are we not obliged to answer, as a matter of course, with a plain, unqualified Yes? It is certainly quite indisputable, that in the sense in which, according to the teaching of Scripture, the testimony of all Christendom, and the belief of the Holy Roman Church, Jesus Christ is the mediator, and the only mediator, no other mediator whatsoever, not even the blessed Virgin, can in any way be in question for us, for our salvation, for our faith. Jesus Christ is in a definite and unambiguous sense the only mediator, beside whom there is no other mediator and no other mediatrix, in the sense in which he

94

is, and is called a mediator. He, namely, as God made man, is the true and only efficient cause of our salvation, as Son of God he is our salvation itself, and access of grace to God the Father. In the unity of his person, he possesses the divine nature as the eternally begotten of the Father, and human nature from the Virgin Mary. He it is, there-fore, who by what he is and what he does, forms the one unique unifying bond between God and his creation that is to be redeemed. In this sense he is the unique mediator.

Nevertheless, we proclaim Mary our mediatrix, spon-taneously, gladly, joyfully, by our prayers, and the honour and trust we show her. The word must therefore have quite a different sense from what it has when, with Holy Scripture, we recognize our Lord as our sole mediator. This use of a word in different senses, (even though the meanings are intrinsically related), has nothing parti-cularly surprising about it. The fact is that human language is poor, it has only a very limited number of words at its disposal. With these few words the whole immense reality of the divine order of salvation has to be expressed, and it has to be referred to again and again, briefly, in few words, without long explanations. Consequently we will always have too few words and too many things to be named. Nobody need be surprised or take offence, then, if we have to use the same word to signify two things as radically different as the mediation of the eternal Word of God made man, and that of the blessed Virgin, who is merely a creature, however endowed with grace she may be. It is only a matter of understanding rightly, each time, what we are saying succinctly, by these few inadequate human words.

If we are to realize how truly the most blessed Virgin can be called our mediatrix, despite the fact that Jesus Christ our Lord is the sole mediator, it is well to remind ourselves first of all, as indeed we did in our first meditation, that we all of us belong together, even in regard to salvation. We therefore have to bear one another's grievous and blessed burden, even when it is a matter of ultimate responsibility, the heavy load of grace, and the direct confrontation with God our saviour and judge. Parents exhort their children, are solicitous for their salvation, and pray for them. Those who teach in the Church proclaim the truths of faith. Priests administer the sacraments of God. We all pray for one another. We all do penance, and bear in common the weight of the guilt of all, just as we have contributed our share to this burden of human guilt. We also belong together in the economy of redemption; we are, as St. Paul once said, God's coadjutors. Each of us is, in a way – how else can one put it? – an intermediary, a mediator of grace for others. Not of course in the sense that we have gone on high to fetch down the saving grace of the eternal God. The grace has to be already there through God's own redemptive operation, for one of us to be able to give it to another. Nor in the sense that we actually produce its effect. But, since it is there, since, in Jesus Christ and in him alone, it has come to us, to the one community of the human race, in which all are interdependent, God in his grace and mercy has also decreed that one should help another, even in the attainment and bestowing of salvation.

God in Jesus Christ has so established grace within the human community's solidarity in history and eternal welfare and loss, that it reaches one member through another, even though in God's perspective, it is intended equally directly for each, in Jesus Christ, the head of the one human race. None of us produces grace, freshly causing something not yet there, bringing it into being. But we are intermediaries and in this sense mediators of grace for each other, and so we shall be held to account before the judgement seat of God, whether, within the measure of our possibilities, in our situation in life, through the gifts and talents we were endowed with, we did for others what we ought to have done, as intermediaries on behalf of our neighbours.

Since this human instrumentality in the communion of saints already exists even on this earth, through the grace of Jesus Christ, how can those who have entered into the glory of God's life, taking their whole life with them – what they were, and do not cease to be – have less importance for us as mediators than they had on earth? Will they not then really attain their full and true importance for us, in that one communion of grace and of the saints, in which they belong together with us? Isn't it precisely these blessed, definitively saved, redeemed human beings who are intermediaries for us, in the full sense? By calling them intermediaries, we do not imply that those who have already attained their salvation in God's eternity, stand between us and the Lord God, any more than we mean that God's ministers on earth do. They are not something that bars our direct access to God, to his grace, and to the one mediator. They are not like the steps involved in bringing a case before a court of appeal, steps that have to be gone through in order to reach eternal providence and the treasure of heavenly grace. They are rather people who stand with us, beside us, in the holy company of the redeemed, bound together in mutual importance for each other, before the eyes of the one God.

God sees us, through the eyes of his creative activity, his grace, and his mercy, as members of a great community. He wills each of us as redeemed, endowed with grace, beloved by him, inasmuch as we belong to this one great holy community, and because we are members of it, and therefore existing also for the sake of the others, who together constitute this one society which receives the grace and mercy of God. To be sure we are always called singly, individually, one by one, by the grace of God, which is always intended precisely for the individual. Nevertheless, unique individuals as we are, we are loved by God only because we belong to all others and because they belong to us. Because God loves them, he loves us, and because he loves us, he loves the others. We cannot dissociate this unity of the creative and salvific will of God, which establishes the unity of grace-endowed humanity. All belong to all, and in a true sense we can say, that all are mediators for all, precisely because the individual is loved by God in as much as he has this innumerable host of brothers and sisters beside him, and is linked to them in the communion of saints. All are intermediaries. We are for all and all are for us. To think otherwise, whether we realize it or not, is to make the kingdom of God, the communion of saints, the eternal church, the kingdom of love, a mere collection of separate individuals, who, in what is of ultimate importance, salvation, have nothing to do with one another. It leaves the individual alone and unaided where it most matters, giving him, contrary to the truth, a redeemer who is not the saviour of all, whereas the real Saviour loved all, and includes each in his love for all, precisely so that each one freed from his isolation, may share in the glory of all.

Consequently it can only be a question of how deeply and radically important one individual is for another, in what way and to what a degree he is a mediator of grace for his brother. Of course there are differences of kind and degree in the matter, for God assigns his grace to each as he wills, including the gift and grace of being a blessing in the salvation of others. So if we now ask what importance as mediatrix the blessed Virgin must have, now that she lives in heaven, adoring the eternal love of the triune God, her life and her heart now perfectly fulfilled, we must reply, that it is impossible to determine or envisage the office of mediatrix that belongs to her, except as being of the same order as her importance was in the divine plan for the history of the earth and mankind and redemption. For, even for her, eternity is the outcome of life here on earth before death. The importance she had in the earthly history of redemption has become valid and irrevocable, precisely because she has entered by death into her ultimate eternal glory and perfection. Now none has had a profounder, more comprehensive function, or one more decisive for the whole divine plan, than the blessed Virgin mother of our Lord Jesus Christ, in the earthly history of redemption, in which there figure, not only the Redeemer, but also the redeemed, not only the Son of God, but also human beings as God's coadjutors, associates. For she received salvation for us, by God's grace, but with true freedom, for us and for our eternal welfare. And what once happened on our behalf through her in that unsurpassable, unique way, must in a true sense have become eternal.

The absolutely unique Yes of consent of the blessed Virgin, which co-operated in determining the whole history of the world, is not a mere happening that has disappeared into the void of the past. It occurred as an event in a personal spiritual history, by grace, and therefore it is – it is eternally. She still utters her eternal Amen, her eternal *Fiat,* Let it be so, Let it be done, to all that God willed, to the whole great ordered plan of redemption, in which we all find place, built up on the foundation which is Christ. She says Amen to it all, because she consented once and for all to Jesus Christ, and because that consent of hers has entered eternity. When God looks upon the one community of the redeemed, and wills each with all the others and because he wills the others, he also looks upon this eternal Yes of the blessed Virgin, the Yes on which he willed, in this order of creation, the salvation of us all, quite directly and absolutely once and for all, to depend. God, therefore, wills our salvation too, in this view of his of Mary as she is in eternal life. When he looks upon her, he sees in her too only the grace of the Word made flesh, and he wills us on her account only because he loves her as the mother of his Son. But because God gives what is his sheer grace to its recipient in such a way that it is truly possessed as the recipient's own, though it still continues inalienably to belong to God and to Christ, this special and individual grace of God is only really recognized and praised when those to whom it is given are aware of it. Such praise does not diminish, but increases the glory of the utter grace of the one mediator. For that reason, therefore, we can truly say of Mary, on account of what she did in the history of redemption, which has become eternal, that in the communion of saints she is the intercessor for all of us, the mediatrix of all graces.

101

We can quietly trust the average Catholic to grasp in his own way and bear in mind in his religious life, the difference there is between the mediation of Christ, and that of the blessed Virgin. He may not be able to express the difference in well-chosen theological concepts, but he knows it. For he knows, and in his prayer applies the fact, that Mary is a created person who has been favoured by grace, and for all the glory of her grace, only a creature. And he knows that Jesus Christ is the Son of God, the eternal Word of the Father, to whom alone in the Father and the Holy Spirit, worship is due. The Catholic is so thoroughly convinced of the divine majesty of his one mediator Jesus Christ, that he is more often in danger of overlooking in Jesus Christ the true man, who has the same nature as we have.

So there is no need for us to be nervous, sparing or niggardly when we honour Mary. It is a sign of a truly Catholic life, when there grows to maturity in our hearts, slowly but genuinely, cultivated humbly and faithfully, a personal and tender love of the blessed Virgin. That is yet another grace that must be prayed for. But since she is the mediatrix who has given us the Lord, since she thereby as intermediary bestows in him and through him all grace, the grace he himself is and the grace he has merited, we must sincerely love and honour her. We must keep on lighting candles on the Maytime altar of our own souls, and the greeting of the angel and Elizabeth in the gospel must rise up in our minds perpetually. "Hail, full of grace, the Lord is with thee; blessed art thou among women; and blessed is the fruit of thy womb!" And we must also repeatedly say: Our Lady, our intercessor, our advocate, reconcile us to your Son, and show us now and after this life, the blessed fruit of your womb; pray for us sinners, now and in the hour of our death. Amen.

MARY

HOLY Virgin, truly mother of the eternal Word who has come into our flesh and our life, Lady who conceived in faith and in your blessed womb the salvation of us all, and so are the mother of all the redeemed, you who live ever in God's life, near to us still, because those united to God are nearest to us.

With the thankfulness of the redeemed, we praise the eternal mercy of God that redeemed you. When your existence began, sanctifying grace already was yours, and that irrevocable grace was with you always. You walked the way of all the children of this earth, the narrow paths which seem to wander so aimlessly through this life of time, commonplace, sorrowful roads, until death. But they were God's ways, the path of faith and unconditional consent: "Be it done unto me according to thy word." And in a moment that never passes, but remains valid for all eternity, your voice became the voice of all mankind, and your Yes was the Amen of all creation to God's irrevocable decree. You conceived in faith and in

your womb him who is at once God and man, creator
and creature, changeless unalterable blessedness, and an
earthly life marked out for bitter death, Jesus Christ our
Lord. For our salvation you said Yes, for us you spoke
your *Fiat*; as a woman of our race you accepted and bore
in your womb and in your love him in whose Name alone
there is salvation in heaven or on earth. Your Yes of
consent ever remained, was never revoked, even when
the course of the life and death of your Son fully revealed
who it was that you had conceived: the Lamb of God,
taking on himself the sins of the world; the Son of Man,
nailed to the Cross by our sinful race's hatred of God, and
thrown, him the Light of the world, into the darkness of
death, the lot that was ours. In you, holy Virgin, who
stood under the Cross of the Redeemer (the real tree of
the knowledge of good and evil, the real tree of life), as the
second Eve and mother of all the living, it was redeemed
humanity, the Church, that stood under the Cross and
received the fruit of redemption and eternal salvation.

Here, virgin and mother, a congregation of the redeemed
and the baptized has now gathered together. Here, then,
where the communion of all the saints is visible and tangible, in this community, we ask you for your intercession. For the communion of saints includes those on
earth and those who have attained their end and perfection, and in it none lives to himself alone. You do not
do so either, then. You pray for all who are linked with
you in this community as redeemed brothers and sisters. So

105

we trustfully request your powerful intercession, which you do not refuse even to those who do not know you. You ask for grace for us to be true Christians: redeemed and baptized, more and more conformed to the life and death of our Lord, living in the Church in its Spirit, worshipping God in spirit and in truth, bearing witness to sanctifying grace through our life in all its branches, as human beings who are pure and chaste, truthful and seeking truth in everything, bravely and humbly giving shape and form to their life as a holy vocation from God, as children of God who, in the words of the apostle, are to "shine as lights in the midst of a crooked and perverse generation" (Phil. 2:15), joyful and confident, their foundation the Lord of all the ages, today and for ever.

We consecrate ourselves to you, holy virgin and mother, because we are consecrated to you. Just as we are not only built up on the corner-stone Jesus Christ but also on the foundation of the apostles and prophets, so too our life and salvation is ever dependent on your consent, on your faith and the fruit of your womb. So when we say that we wish to be consecrated to you, we are only proclaiming our willingness to be, and to accept in mind and heart and action both interior and external, what we really are. By such a consecration we are only making the attempt to carry out in our own life-history the plan of redemption God laid down and in which he has already made his dispositions for us.

We come to you, then, because in you our salvation

came to be, was conceived by you. Since we are conse-crated to you thereby, and are consecrating ourselves to you, show to us who have been made sharers in your grace, Jesus the blessed fruit of thy womb. Show to us Jesus our Lord and Saviour, the light of truth and the advent of God into this world of time. Show to us Jesus who has truly suffered and truly risen, who is the Son of the Father and the son of earth, because your Son. Show to us him in whom we are truly set free from all prin-cipalities and powers that are still under heaven, even though the man of earth is still subject to them. Show us Jesus Christ, yesterday, today and for ever. Hail Mary, full of grace . . . Amen.